AF249421

PRAISE FOR A FUTURE UNTOLD

If you want to change, you need to think deeply about storytelling. This lovely, elegant book will set you off on that journey.

— *Johann Hari, author of NY Times bestsellers* Chasing the Scream *and* Lost Connections

I have long resisted all efforts to blame failed narratives for our collective woes, but Alina Siegfried has convinced me that the hero's journey may have applications beyond the next Jedi movie. For if we can't imagine and articulate a story better than capitalism's myth of exponential growth, we will indeed play out this one to its awful conclusion. There is another, untold story of our future, and this is our first best effort at helping us tell it together.

— *Douglas Rushkoff, documentarian, media theorist, and author of* Team Human, Present Shock, *and* Throwing Rocks at the Google Bus: How Growth Became the Enemy of Prosperity

Alina Siegfried guides the reader on a trek that is challenging, both intellectually and emotionally. The journey begins with a compelling diagnosis of current threats to the future of planet Earth and its inhabitants. She navigates us through the various contributions that have led to this bleak situation, including political systems, the media, various business models and basic human psychology. But the journey is lightened by her clear and frank prose. We are lifted by her poetry which marks key points along the route and her stories telling of her life, family, experiences and travels. Ultimately she guides us to a place of hope for the future. Here she gives us 10 new narratives – new ways of looking at the world which she suggests will halt the global risk and regenerate both the physical world and our societal connections. I found very compelling her kind and thorough analysis of the need to rethink how we view our enemies and those with whom we have fundamental disagreement. She sheds light one of the most difficult problems facing modern diplomacy. Our systems for managing threats to international peace and security have lost touch with the collective approach embodied in the United Nations. Too often states are reluctant to listen to other perspectives and too quick to demonise opponents. This is another of our current systemic weaknesses and another reason why Alina Siegfried's *A Future Untold* is so timely.

— Colin Keating, former New Zealand Ambassador to the UN and President of the UN Security Council

In this book, Alina Siegfried argues that the world is shaped by stories, for better or for worse. In poetry and anecdote, she explores the power of different narratives to create or destroy. A wise and hopeful work, it offers ten new myths as a gift to the future. He taonga aroha – a treasure that radiates generosity of spirit.

— Dame Anne Salmond, Order of Merit of New Zealand, anthropologist, and Distinguished Professor at University of Auckland

Solving global problems with collaborative narratives will require new goals, strategies, and methods. Alina Siegfried leads the way to reclaiming our faith in humanity by showing us how to escape the moral distress we feel when competitive reasoning causes so much harm.

— *Annette Simmons, author of* The Story Factor

A remarkable synthesis of a multitude of well established traditions and practices, on the one hand, and emergent, technology driven trends, on the other. All grounded in deeply personal experiences. It is an inspired call and a practical guide to a different future - more prosperous and equitable. A Future Untold is simultaneously... smart and accessible, eye-opening and multi-disciplinary, a broad survey of trends inflected with anecdotes rich in meaning. It is sober in analysis of the scale of our challenges and while remaining deeply optimistic in spirit.

— *Jee Kim, founding former Chief Executive Officer, Narrative Initiative*

I loved this book. Look around, the world is burning, the rest is in flood, we have a plague raging around us, locusts are doing their thing.... and yet we are surrounded by everyday heroes, majestic landscapes, reliant nature and exquisite beauty. How do we balance fearless compassion and love for all life while looking after ourselves and channeling our rage into hope? Alina's book helped me to reconnect with the stories that bind us, and how all real change comes from a narrative first - we are in such need of storytellers who can help us navigate to the futures we want. Data and science won't get us to a better, more hopeful future - but narratives of our joint futures that give us hope, a sense of purpose and paths to follow will. This book is for anyone who wants to make a better future inevitable.

— *Melissa Clark-Reynolds, Officer of the NZ Order of Merit, serial entrepreneur*

A Future Untold is filled with truth and grace. A powerful re-frame for anyone working on global change and social transformation. It's a poignant and deep exploration of how stories and meta-narratives shape business, society, and the future we create. Alina Siegfried balances the deftness of a poet with practical examples drawn from the worlds of tech innovation, social change, and sustainability. It's a rare feat that gently invites you as a fish to see the water — and further beckons you into a bigger story you can inhabit outside the fishbowl. This book provides a powerful and compelling invitation into the subtle yet infinite power of framing and language for creating more of the better future and healthier world we all want. A delightful debut from a storyteller who knows her stuff.

— *Michael Margolis, Founder and Chief Executive Officer, Storied, and Author of* Story 10x: Turn the Impossible Into the Inevitable

This evocative, perceptive, and beautiful book is about us and the living Earth. To tell the story, Alina beautifully weaves her moving memoir – of a life lived in deep and rich connection with others and nature –

into an inspiring guide to our collective future. Alina's wisdom will up-end your life, giving you courage to grow richer, deeper relationships with people and planet...beginning by learning "the subtle art of story listening."

— *Rod Oram, Business Journalist*

Heartfelt, incisive, compassionate, strategic and above all deeply wise, *A Future Untold* offers an outstanding guide for campaigners, change makers and citizens on how to navigate this moment of crisis and creation. Alina Siegfried moves seamlessly from personal to global and from cutting edge to timeless, exploring how stories create our reality as much as they describe it, and setting out a compelling set of ten new myths that can help bring about a breakthrough rather than breakdown future. A superb work that will be read for years to come.

— Alex Evans, Author of The Myth Gap, *and Founder,*
Larger Us

This is a book about being called by the power of story. Alina is committed to the ability of storytelling to reshape our understanding of the world and so, through our actions, to reshape the world itself. And she tells the stories she is carrying with the energy and joy of the spoken word poet that she is.

— Dougald Hine, Co-founder of the Dark Mountain Project
and A School Called HOME

A FUTURE UNTOLD

Copyright © 2021 Alina Siegfried

Alina Siegfried asserts her moral right to be identified as the author of this work.

All rights reserved. No part of this publication may be produced or transmitted in any form or by any means, electronic or mechanical, including photocopying, recording or information storage and retrieval systems, without permission in writing from the copyright holder.

Published by Systemic

alinasiegfried.com

A catalogue record for this book is available from the National Library of New Zealand.

ISBN 978-0-473-58746-8 (paperback)

ISBN 978-0-473-58747-5 (EPUB)

Cover design: Peter Roband

CONTENTS

This book is dedicated to Taika, Frankie, and all the other children who will inherit the world that we shape in the coming decades

FOREWORD

As these lines are written, we are experiencing the third, and in some parts of the world the fourth, wave of the COVID-19 pandemic. A zoonotic disease caused by a spill-over of virus from wild animals, potentially via an intermediary host (e.g., livestock), to us humans. Something went wrong in one corner of the planet and it abruptly knocked out the entire world, with devastating effects on human life, jobs and the economy.

But SARS-CoV-2 was not a black swan; it was no surprise. On the contrary, the pandemic is an expected manifestation of this age of the Anthropocene. Simply, it is what we should expect to face 70 years after we embarked on the great acceleration, the advent of the Anthropocene, which has brought us to our current predicament. Overexploitation of natural wildlife habitats, risky hunting and trade of wildlife, and unsustainable livestock and agricultural practices, colliding with a hyper-connected and globalised world of transport and trade. It is, well, in short, a perfect cocktail for a pandemic. One that has caused a global health crisis, which interacts with the global climate crisis, both of which are tightly connected with the global ecological crisis.

And the red thread? Overall, that things are changing faster and in a more unexpected and abrupt way than we had anticipated. As I write in mid-2021, a freak heatwave is hitting British Columbia and US West Coast, with 49.6°C experienced in Lytton, BC—which after a few days, burned down to the ground. A few days ago, the World Meteorological Organization confirmed the hottest temperature ever recorded on Antarctica, 18.3°C (recorded February 6, 2020). In the Arctic, the summer of 2020 hit parts of Siberia with temperatures of 38°C, accelerating the thawing of permafrost. Science now shows that the Arctic summer ice, several ice sheets in West Antarctica, and tropical coral reef systems, have crossed or are very close to crossing tipping points of no return. Extreme weather events hit more frequently and harder. All this at 1.25°C of global warming. And in a few decades, if we fail to turn things around, we are bound to commit all future generations to global warming exceeding 2°C, a place that we have not experienced for the last 3 million years. This is our predicament. It is on our watch, the adult generation alive on Earth today, that all this has happened. Scientifically, we can conclude, this is a planetary emergency.

And what do we do when faced with emergencies? We rise. We transform, solve the problem, and move rapidly to safe ground. We urgently need a global transformation back within our safe operating space—a world that develops and provides prosperity and equity within planetary boundaries. To succeed we need solutions. Scalable and affordable solutions. But perhaps most importantly, we need a new narrative. A narrative that helps us to deviate away from potentially catastrophic risks, and transform the world in harmony with our home, planet Earth.

And this is where I, as a scientist, connect wholeheartedly with Alina. She states early in the book that "the world is built on stories". I cannot agree more. And largely, I am afraid, it is overwhelmingly built on the wrong story—so far. A story of infinite economic growth, consumption, and production, as if we lived on an infinite planet. In all fairness, this story worked reasonably well, for as long as the Earth system hosted plentiful wildlife on land, forests, soils, and fish in the ocean. As long as the atmosphere, groundwater, and stratosphere could absorb human pollutants without sending invoices back to our societies.

But quite recently, in my assessment sometime around the mid 1980s to 1990s, we came to the end of the road of this planetary free-ride. There was no more room for greenhouse gases in the atmosphere. No more capacity in the biosphere to absorb pollutants and nutrients. No more fish to overexploit. No more natural ecosystems to degrade and destroy. For decades now, have we been in a state of mismatch between the dominant story of our lives which sees us exploiting and polluting for free without consequence, and the urgency to reboot and follow the path of a new story where we reconnect to our blue little marble.

Who knows, as Alina suggests, perhaps for a brief moment in 1968 we had the opportunity to recalibrate our relationship with planet Earth. Earthrise from Apollo 8 provided us world citizens with a deep existential shock. Is she so small, merely a beautiful little blue marble, clearly alone and vulnerable? But alas, we never deviated from the industrial highway. Instead oblivious to unintended consequences, to quote Alina's "Big World, Small Planet: The Remix" poem, we paved freeways across the future and built stronger and stronger combustion engines for our industrial metabolism.

And here we are, in dire need of a new narrative. A narrative that we need to advance as we walk—no, run—along exponential roadmaps, phasing out fossil fuels, transitioning to sustainable food systems, and building up circular regenerative consumption and production processes. The beauty in all of this, what gives us a sliver of hope, is that the emerging narrative is so compelling, and increasingly not only maturing but also loaded with evidence.

Sustainability is no longer a question of protecting the environment from human abuse, or a question of how much we need to sacrifice for the sake of our economic development. Today, sustainability is emerging as the determining factor whether we succeed or fail as a species.

This is our renaissance moment, in a world that must transition to the next level of modernity, where the health of people and the health of the planet not only go hand in hand, but provide outcomes for jobs, the economy, equity, security, health, stability, and peace. It is time for a new story.

Johan Rockström
Professor in Earth System Science
Director Potsdam Institute for Climate Impact Research
July 4, 2021

ABOUT THIS BOOK

Throughout my late twenties and early thirties, I had a gnawing feeling that each turn in my winding career was taking me further down a path towards professional obscurity. My high school career counsellor had given me the impression that once you picked a vocation, that was it. We were given stark warnings not to have long, unexplained periods on our résumé where we weren't working at a job that pointed up a ladder somewhere, lest we be deemed as unfocused or lacking in commitment. I had a fair amount of anxiety about changing my focus frequently, but just couldn't help myself—I was just so interested in so many different things.

The chapters in the story of my life are as varied as they are many. Each career move, location, relationship, significant life event, and phase of life has added to my ever-accumulating pile of anecdotes, reflections, titbits, and little nuggets of insight into how we tell stories. The past fifteen years of my storytelling career have taken me through the deep listening work of engaging with communities on resource management and environmental work, and into the belly of the beast of political campaign messaging. I emerged out the other side into tech start-ups, crowdfunding, and framing a brighter future through bringing to life the stories of global changemakers. Eleven of those fifteen years have seen me embracing vulnerability and sharing my own stories with crowds of strangers in the form of spoken word poetry. Since winning the New Zealand National Poetry Slam in 2012, my spoken word has struck a chord with senior government officials at conferences as readily as it has with activists holding banners at climate change rallies.

Over time I have come to view the twists and turns in my career not as a weakness, but rather as a great strength for a couple of reasons. Firstly, they have allowed me to intersect with many diverse and varied sectors of society, hear different people's stories, and understand their perspectives and their views of the world. I have strived to become adept not just at storytelling, but also story-listening. I've swapped tales of bravado at the local dive bar with the construction crew I worked on in prairie Canada, and heard the back stories of New Zealand members of Parliament. Long before documenting the journeys of world-leading systems change entrepreneurs and impact investors, I planted strawberries in the rain in Switzerland with Polish immigrants. For a few months, I slummed it out living in a cheap tent at a $4-a-night fruit-pickers camp in British Columbia's Okanagan Valley, talking with people who had fallen through society's cracks as the November snows began to settle on the ground. My journey has been enriched by listening carefully to the tales of everyone I've met along the way.

Being exposed to many diverse communities and perspectives increases our chances of being able to communicate effectively in different cultural languages. It means being able to serve as a bridge between divergent schools of thought, factions of society, and different industries and sectors. It means being able to see the gaps in one particular way of thinking, and how the glue from another way might patch those gaps to provide a more complete picture of both problems and solutions.

The second reason I view my winding journey as a good thing is because it has given me a much clearer view of the interconnected nature of the various natural, social, cultural, and built systems upon which the world operates. Rather than considering problems in a siloed way, as I may have been tempted to do earlier in my career, I now look for the many interdependent, dynamic elements and influences. The biggest challenges that we face as a global society arise out of broken systems. To solve them, we need to take a systemic approach.

My first great love was the natural world, thanks to many early formative memories exploring the wild with my Swiss father who was drawn to the mountains, and my Kiwi mother who preferred gentle walks through the native New Zealand bush. Perhaps as a natural progression of this upbringing, much of my career has gravitated towards resource management and environmental advocacy. So my first thought for this book was to address storytelling and narrative to support environmental issues such as climate change, freshwater pollution, biodiversity loss, and the declining health of the oceans. But I have come to realise that the truth of transformative systems change is that we cannot separate the social from the environmental. The current degraded state of our natural environments is not so much an ecological problem, as it is a social and cultural one. It is our beliefs, our habits, our laws, our social institutions, and our economic structures that are at the root of our environmental woes. Additionally, for many millions who are struggling just to survive day to day, worrying about the environment is a luxury and privilege they cannot afford. The reality is that the destinies of the planet's natural ecosystems, the life that inhabits them, and the humans who have spread across the globe are all intricately intertwined and interdependent. So in order to solve environmental problems we need social action to bring everyone with us, and we need cultural change to help us reorient the status quo of how we live on the planet. At the root of cultural change is changing the wide-reaching narratives that underpin our understanding of "the way things are."

I believe that stories are the most powerful force on this planet to enact change. Stories have the capacity to evoke empathy and inspire action in a way that logic and reason cannot. Stories have the power to inspire revolution and topple empires. Equally so, stories have built the status quo. Our collective, inherited cultural stories and narratives surrounding money, governance, people, how we got to be here, the meaning of life, and our relationship with the natural world form the foundations upon which we've built our social systems. Everything around us is built upon a collective adherence or active rejection of deep cultural myths informed by social psychology, the political climate, social norms, and myriad other factors. And so it follows that storytelling holds the key to changing these guiding narratives and myths, and rerouting the trajectory of the future along with them.

This is not a how-to book. If you are looking for a step-by-step guide on how to tell good stories, then this is probably not the book for you. If, however, you have a feeling deep inside that all is not well with the current trajectory of our world, and you wish to understand the role of stories in building a world that better aligns with your vision of the future, then you have come to the right place. This book is for those who prescribe to the fundamental premise that we can do better. I present it as a living collection of stories and learnings from my life and career, and from those I have intersected with over the years. It is a story in itself about how I have witnessed the ability of storytelling to shift the needle on the broad, overarching narratives and guiding myths that inform our lives. This is what I know how to do. I am a storyteller.

Similarly, this is not so much a self-help book as it is a collective help book. In places, the focus might be on examining your own stories, and in this regard much of the work that there is to do is personal. The narratives that guide families, communities, organisations, and nations are intricately intertwined with the stories of the individuals within those groups. When we consider that each of us is a singular thread in a complex, interwoven pattern that makes up the tapestry of life, we can begin to see how changing our stories can sway the collective narratives that guide us. When enough threads in the tapestry change colour, it begins to take on a new form, a new pattern, uncovering a new and beautiful roadmap forward.

I offer this book as an invitation into conversation about the role of story in transformational change, drawing from my own experiences. Yours will be different, and that's okay. At times I may challenge your thinking. At times you may disagree with me. That's okay too. We don't need to agree, but I believe that what we do need is to listen and understand each other a whole lot better. If you do find yourself challenged, I invite you to sit with that discomfort and take the time to gently probe and investigate why you disagree. I encourage you to keep an open mind. Dig deep. Don't be afraid to question the things you have always taken for granted. Don't shy away from examining the stories you hold most dear, about yourselves or others. It is in fearlessly digging deep, being vulnerable with yourself, and approaching things with non-judgmental curiosity that transformative change begins.

The book is laid out to take you from the micro to the macro of storytelling and narrative. Section 1 explores the nuts and bolts of storytelling and explains why it is so crucial in helping to address the defining challenges of our time. Section 2 covers framing and the stories themselves, the tales we tell and yarns we spin to capture hearts and imaginations. In Section 3, I investigate the levers we need to pull to shift many of the predominant narratives we have come to assume as a given in our everyday lives. In the final section, I offer ten new guiding myths for humanity that can serve as beacons towards a more regenerative, just, and equitable world. Because the book is part memoir and because I build upon concepts and stories introduced earlier, you'll get the most out of it if you read the chapters in sequential order, as they are best understood with the context of prior chapters in mind. In saying that, I have also tried to write the chapters in such a way that they will still make sense if you choose to dive in and out.

In the initial stages of planning this book, I had hoped to travel to the far reaches of the globe and hear from different leaders and communities about how the power of story had resulted in significant positive change or a shift in the status quo. However, as borders began to shut down as COVID-19 swept the globe, and it became clear that international travel was not going to be possible for quite some time, I was forced to look at Plan B— connecting and collecting stories through fibre optic and copper cables, and via satellites orbiting above our heads. It was perhaps quite fitting for a book about storytelling for change that I had to deviate from a system of travel that would have seen me racking up many thousands of carbon miles to meet with people in person. I'm the first to admit that video conferencing is a poor substitute for the visceral, somatic experience of sitting face to face with someone as they share pieces of themselves with you. But given the circumstances, it's an amusing irony that I have been forced to take my own medicine.

COVID-19 has shaken up many of our long-held assumptions about virtually every aspect of our life, from how we work and travel to our economic system's reliance on international trade. The disruption is set to continue for some time, and the pandemic is far from the only threat to our deep-seated stories about "the way things are." In this time of increasing political instability, a rise in populism across a number of countries, and many ecological systems already in collapse, old stories are breaking apart around us every week. While it is painful, it also represents an opportunity for us to chart a new course for humanity—one that is kinder, more understanding, filled with more joy, and that serves to support all life on Earth, human or otherwise. Through our words and actions, we choose to build the world we want to live in. What we do now will matter for decades. We need flexibility, blue-sky thinking, moral imagination, an attitude of possibility, and a return to core values. We could even benefit from adopting a child-like naivety about what might be possible if we dare imagine things that many believe can never happen. Our global systemic challenges are overwhelmingly complex. With that in mind, I suggest that what we need going forward is not so much a map, but rather a compass. With all the myriad factors at play, we really don't know what the future looks like and what kind of terrain we might encounter. But with a firm idea of at least the direction in which we wish to journey together, we have a chance of getting to where we want to be. Our stories can serve as our compass to help us stay the course.

No matter what your day job, your profession, your vocation, or passion, you are a storyteller, whether you like it or not. Just as I am uncomfortable with the notion that Artists (with a capital A) are separate from the general population of humans, the same is true of us as storytellers. We are all artists and we are all storytellers in an active relationship with our stories; they are always morphing, changing, and growing.

As outlined in the late science fiction author Ursula Le Guin's 1986 essay, "The Carrier Bag Theory of Fiction",[1] the future story of humanity will not be that of the hero wielding weapons against the problems of the world. No, it will rather be the collection of many uplifting and life-sustaining stories that are gathered together in a carrier bag of sorts, a container. Let this book be one of those containers. There is a certain power and beauty in the invitation to craft new stories of better futures, and to recognise the agency that we have in making a conscious choice about which sorts of stories we live out daily. We can and we must re-author the social, political, and economic systems that we have built to better serve us and the planet. The survival of all life as we know it depends upon it. Most of all though, we need to listen to the stories of others with respect and grace, and to tell our own in ways that inspire hope, build bridges, and pave the way to the more beautiful future that we never dreamed possible. This story is mine; I hope you enjoy it.

~ Alina

THE WHOLE WORLD IS A STORY

1

A POET'S EPIPHANY

It was a late winter evening on the Canadian prairies in a local bar called Lydia's. Snow still on the ground and the wind whipping up Saskatoon's Broadway Avenue, some 150 people had escaped the cold to have their hearts and minds warmed by the words brewing inside. From behind the safety of glaring stage lights, a microphone, and a pint of Dutch courage, my journey innocuously began into the power of storytelling, narrative, and the spoken word. As I began to speak, a nascent form of rhyme and metre began to fall from my lips. I played with the resonance within my mouth. I held the words like a savoured first bite, bursting with flavour, yet eager to let the poetry flow forth. I spoke far too quickly, having made the rookie mistake of trying to fit too many words and concepts into my first attempt at penning a poem for the stage, and knowing that I was butting up against the three-minute limit for a poetry slam performance.

The event was called Tonight It's Poetry, and I had found my kin. Every Sunday night, this ragtag bunch of poets, writers, lovers, dreamers, bards, and enthusiastic spectators would gather together and share words in the form of poetry. It was a welcoming community, with everyone encouraged heartily to share their words of truth and entertainment. The polar opposite of comedy gigs, where the audience typically treats a struggling performer with heckling and awkward, stony silences, this community would instead loudly encourage a poet who had lost their words, with snapping fingers to break the silence or even someone shouting back their last spoken words to jog their memory. Sometimes it was a small gathering, other times a rowdy crowd that lingered far beyond what is reasonable on a work night. Sombre tales of grief and heartbreak were interspersed with joyous celebrations, modern-day philosophy, musings on the current state of the world/country/city, and heartfelt accounts of unravelling personal lives. Occasionally the odd random stranger would amble in off the street, seeking respite from the cold and some music in what was a gig bar every other night of the week. It was always fun to watch them propped up at the bar, their expression changing from confusion to amusement, occasional discomfort, and then eventually to awe and reverence. On quieter evenings, the atmosphere was one of intimacy, as if we were telling each other our most vulnerable secrets and by exposing them, setting them free. My friend and fellow poet Phil Kaye says that spoken word is like therapy, except that instead of paying a professional to listen to your problems, the audience pays you for the privilege of hearing them. Living half a world away from my home in New Zealand, I had been seeking belonging, and I found it amongst this diverse group of brave souls prepared to share their stories.

I had been going to Tonight It's Poetry for several months before I entered my first poetry slam. The slam was a more structured affair than the standard open mic nights, in which poets would vie for the title of slam champion in a competitive arena of words and wit. With enforced time limits and without the aid of costumes, music, or props, poets performed their original poetry to the crowd, among which were five judges holding scorecards. The judges were selected at random by the MC that evening, in an attempt to democratise the act of artistic critique. Simply by making the effort to show up that evening, any stranger could be deemed worthy of deciding what was and what wasn't good poetry. It was the ultimate challenge to the high-brow poetry elite, and I instantly fell in love with the rough, raw, ridiculous, and anarchistic nature of it all.

I was keen to enter and had been thinking a lot about what I could write a poem about. At that time, I was working for a provincial-level environmental NGO, advocating for the protection of freshwater resources and running a public education campaign on water conservation. To find out first-hand what it felt like to be severely water-limited, I decided to embrace a month-long personal water conservation challenge that saw me using no more than 25 litres of water per day to meet all my daily needs—drinking, cooking, bathing, laundry, flushing the toilet—everything. At that time, the research indicated that the average Canadian was using 230 litres of water per day, so the challenge involved slashing my water use by almost 90 percent. Showers were out, sponge baths were in. I used my grey water from bathing and laundry to flush the toilet and recorded all my water use in a notebook. I blogged and vlogged about my experiences, sharing the challenges and frustrations that arose. Laundry was a particularly long, drawn-out affair that took up most of my Sunday afternoons. As I experienced the challenges of living with much reduced access to water, it struck me that this topic could make for a unique and engaging poem. So, throughout the month I jotted down various lines of poetry, and on March 28, 2010, I entered my first poetry slam. Despite my nerves and rushed delivery, I came in fourth out of a field of twelve poets. Not bad for a first attempt, I told myself.

The real magic, however, was to unfold in the following weeks. At subsequent poetry evenings or sometimes even out in public, people who had been in the audience that first night would come up to me and proudly tell me about the ways in which they were now saving water. They were turning off the tap while brushing their teeth and using lower water use settings in their washing machine. One particularly excited woman even approached me in the street, wearing a power suit that looked like it cost more than my first car, and told me that she was now collecting her excess shower water in a bucket to water her houseplants. An untitled poem at the time of first performance, it eventually became known simply as "The Water Poem," by virtue of the number of times people referred to it as such. I was blown away with how folks had been inspired to act by hearing a simple poem. I had achieved a kind of cut-through in three minutes behind a microphone that I had been failing to achieve through the dry and boring PowerPoint presentations of my day job. The light bulb that went on in my mind in the weeks following that performance was the first realisation of many as I began to understand the power of an authentic story, in this case packaged up as a poem. While the modern poetry slam format may be relatively new, launched in 1984 in Chicago by a blue-collar worker called Marc Kelly Smith, the roots of competitive poetry go back much further. In Ancient Greece, poetry and other literary events featured heavily at athletic festivals, with celebrity poets fiercely battling it out for glory. Rich reward was bestowed upon those who won, while punishment for subpar poems could mean the crowd turning on the offending poet or even beating them up. Between 1912 and 1948, poetry even featured as a medal-winning event at the Olympic Games.

My storytelling awakening in 2010 came at a time when I was cutting my teeth in the arena of communications for change. Following a couple of years of travel that had seen me driving across Canada from the Yukon to the northern tip of Newfoundland, I had settled in Saskatoon, the largest city in the prairie province of Saskatchewan. After an unexpected yet rewarding career tangent rolling up my sleeves in the construction industry, I returned to my resource management roots and took on a role with a leading provincial NGO focused on protecting the province's expansive and diverse environment. I became familiar with the various issues and complexities surrounding the use of freshwater resources on the prairies.

The southern half of Saskatchewan is dominated by ever-stretching fields of grain crops with the occasional pocket of rolling grassland; the northern half, a sparsely populated wilderness of lakes, wetlands, and boreal forest, home to bears, moose, elk, caribou, beavers, lynx, and other species of quintessentially Canadian wildlife. The bitterly cold winters, cold enough to freeze your eyelashes together, were contrasted by the drought-prone summers. Agriculture and industry competed for freshwater use in a province rich in various minerals—uranium, gold, oil, and potash, which is used in fertiliser. Throwing myself into advocacy work, I intersected with freshwater leaders from across the country representing a diversity of interests. I took a crash course in values-based campaign storytelling and social marketing, learning of the power and potency of human networks to spread new ideas. And yet, there was a dissonance between what I was learning and the effect that I felt I was having in my day-to-day work. My messages were not landing as well as I had hoped, and I seldom had any feedback that my efforts were actually helping people to make better use of water.

Upon writing and performing "The Water Poem," something shifted in me. The difference was that I had made our relationship to fresh water personal and tangible. I shared the story of my anguish at spilling my bucket of bathing water after a long day of work, meaning that I not only lost a good chunk of my day's water allowance, but also that I had to go back to the stove to heat up another batch of water; the time it took to get the tap running hot was water down the drain that I couldn't afford. It was the kind of visceral experience that cannot be replicated when you're telling someone in an abstract way how many litres of water they can save by installing a low-flow tap in their kitchen. Having learned a great deal about global water politics and inequity of access, I had also woven in the story of an anonymous woman walking on a dusty road with a clay jug, representing the millions around the world who need to travel many miles daily to fetch the water they and their families need to stay alive. This added another layer to the narrative of the poem—not my own, but one that I hoped people could empathise with. The piece ends on the poignant note that water makes up a great deal of our body mass; we are literally made of water. The result of all these stories as told together was a short, yet multi-dimensional tale that struck a chord on a cognitive, emotional, and spiritual level.

The world is built on stories. We humans have crafted collective stories that inform every aspect of our social and anthropological systems. Look around you. Maybe you are lying on your bed enjoying some evening reading before going to sleep. You might be sitting in a cafe. Perhaps you're on the bus, on your way to work. In any of these situations, collectively derived human stories are never far away. Your bedroom, presumably in a house or apartment you may or may not share with a few other humans, is the result of a cultural story that tells us it is the norm to sleep in a segregated space from others who live around you. It is a cultural story that values privacy, seclusion, and respite from the world. A cafe is the result of a cultural story that speaks to people's desire to socialise (and caffeinate), in an ambient atmosphere with music, mood lighting, and conversational buzz. In part, the existence of buses is based on the narrative that time is scarce, and that it is better to travel somewhere at speed, rather than at the pace that our own two legs could carry us. And if you are indeed travelling to your workplace, there are dozens of cultural stories surrounding the concept of work itself. Stories of bosses and subordinates. Stories of what constitutes productive and unproductive time. The story that humans need to exchange mental or physical labour in order to gather the transferrable currency to buy or rent a house with a bedroom, enjoy a coffee or a muffin at a favourite local cafe, and purchase a bus ticket. I'm not arguing against any of these systems. I love coffee, travel, and my bedroom. But the fact remains that we— humans, that is—made all of this stuff up. We built every aspect of the anthropogenic world.

If we look around at the modern world, much of what we have collectively built is pretty mind-blowing. The keyboard I'm typing this on, making words instantly appear on the screen I'm staring at. The vaccines that we have created to protect us from communicable diseases and viruses. The fact that I can instantly see and talk with someone on the other side of the world in real time on a video call, thanks to the satellites that we have placed in orbit with the help of rockets propelled by hydrocarbons and chemicals mined from beneath the surface of the Earth. Through human creativity, innovation, cooperation, and a set of shared cultural stories, we have achieved some pretty incredible things. But we have also done some pretty awful things. Our economic and geopolitical systems have created vast inequalities between different populations and communities. Our inherited cultural narratives surrounding gender have perpetuated varying degrees of discrimination against half of the world's population. We have destabilised the climate system of an entire planet. Systemic stories surrounding race, ethnicity, religion, and political views have built metaphorical walls between us, further reinforcing our ideas of who is "us" and who is "them." In some cases, those stories have even constructed physical walls.

Because all of our human-built systems are built on stories, the key to changing them lies in rewriting those stories. If we are to have a chance at solving complex global challenges like poverty, hunger, disease, inequality, systemic racism, climate change, biodiversity loss, ocean acidification, and political polarisation, we need to re-author the predominant narratives that have allowed these problems to arise in the first place. And to do that we must first understand how our human minds succumb to the mechanics of story.

2

____

THE DNA OF STORY

EVER SINCE THE FIRST SEEDS OF COGNITIVE INTENTION SURFACED and manifested themselves as grunts, gestures, and eye contact between prehistoric individuals, humans have been telling stories. As we gathered around fires for warmth, stories became the vehicle by which we built relationships, entertained, derived meaning, and transmitted vital information to each other. Stories have always been how we make sense of the world. They are the operating system upon which human beings are programmed, informing how we organise our lives and societies and acting as the delivery agents of culture. Stories engage both our hearts and our minds, driving our behaviour in ways that are largely subconscious to us. They tell us who is a part of our tribe, and who is not. They tell us what is a normal and acceptable way to behave, and what sort of behaviours will see us being socially shunned. They prescribe the consequences that come from certain actions, and they teach us lessons.

When we were young children, we were master storytellers. We invented the world around us, limited only by the confines of our own imagination. Our stories were cherished treasures and we devoured them with relish. Whether they were our favourite books, the stories we learned from teachers and community leaders, the ones we made up, or the funny stories we heard our parents tell about us time and again, our stories were the markers that helped us orient ourselves and our growing sense of identity in the world. They showed us the way and we felt their power strongly. Then somewhere along the path from childhood into adulthood, many of us have lost our belief in the magic of stories. Humanity might look at ourselves collectively and think that us clever humans have triumphed over our primal minds, with our evolved level of rational analysis, which has taken the place of myth, intuition, and story. Yet these vehicles of knowledge transferral hold innate power, and whether we are conscious of it or not, stories still hold a great deal of sway over us. We have not succeeded in changing the human mind so much as we have tipped the balance of what sort of information we value. We rarely afford story a defined place at the decision-making table, relying instead on the reasoned, the proven, the objective, scientific truth. Yet we forget that we are, at our core, messy, irrational creatures who are swayed by story much more readily than we are swayed by fact.

When I wrote "The Water Poem," without realising it I had crafted a short story that made use of framing, story, narrative, and myth—four siblings within the broad family of storytelling that drive the development of culture. Working together to inform our day-to-day feelings and behaviours, they paint a picture of how we interpret the world. Like most siblings, they have moments where they get on splendidly, while at other times they are in conflict. They are constantly in motion and shaping each other. Our choice of language and the way we frame things influences the tone of the stories that we tell, which in turn influences high-level narratives. If we are to think of narrative as a mosaic, then stories are the tiles within that mosaic, and frames are the hues and patterns contained within the tiles. Perhaps myths are whatever it is that we feel or interpret when we stand back and look at the mosaic as a whole. This chapter takes a look at each of these four elements, and how they affect our everyday lives. Note that I sometimes use the terms *story*, *narrative*, and *myth* interchangeably in this book, as they are closely related and are context-dependent.

———

At the very foundation of storytelling is language, and we cannot make use of language without *framing*. Frames are mental structures, ideas, or concepts that help us to make sense of the world around us. They are the cognitive shortcuts and metaphors that we use to provide instant context and information about any given matter. We use frames hundreds of times a day in everyday conversation, media, politics, education, and advertising. Slogans, taglines, and political catchcries rely on frames. The memes you see in your social media feeds rely on frames. They provide snapshots that in a microsecond draw on mental patterns, stereotypes, and heuristics (mental shortcuts) to provide meaning or understanding with just one or a handful of words.

Frames gain strength through repetition: the more we hear a certain frame, the more it becomes our accepted version of reality. Think of the term *natural resources*. Most of us use this phrase without a second thought, yet it implicitly suggests that the gifts of the natural world are there for humans to take and use. It doesn't frame them as part of a whole complex living system or provide any clue that if we do in fact remove these "resources," that the integrity of the living system suffers.

Through our choice of language, we are reinforcing a narrative of human dominance over nature. Consequently, we are heading down a path where we are consuming natural ecosystems on this planet as if we had another one to move to. When we are exposed to frames, they do not land on a blank slate. The readiness with which we accept or reject any given frame depends on many different factors. From the values and morals we hold most dear, to our relationships, beliefs, and early experiences of childhood, our minds are programmed to assess and categorise the information coming at us. We accept or ignore new information depending on how it is framed, and whether or not it fits with our pre-existing views about the world and how we see ourselves within it.

The most important and familiar part of storytelling, stories themselves capture our hearts and minds from a young age. They are the conduits by which we gain understanding and find meaning. Usually we tell stories to serve or fulfil some predetermined purpose—to inspire, educate, entertain, inform, persuade, or manipulate. The word *author* is from the Latin word *auctus*, which translates literally to "one who causes to grow." As such, our stories may sometimes take on a mythic quality with some sort of moral lesson or symbolic meaning attached, such as those that lie behind fables and parables.

Often when I put my young son to bed, he asks me to tell him a story. Not to read him a story, but to invent one on the spot. One evening I pulled a story out of the depths of my imagination about a snail called Hieronymus who had lost his shell, so he slithered into a pumpkin and found a seed to act as a new shell. It was a ridiculous and whimsical tale and one that I proceeded to forget about five minutes later. Yet a week later at bedtime, while I was in the middle of telling a new story, my son interjected with a comment about Hieronymus and his pumpkin seed shell. Putting aside the amusement I felt at hearing a four-year-old attempting to say "Hieronymus," I was surprised that such a fantastical tale that I had whipped out of thin air was still occupying his thoughts and imagination a week later. But we all do this, whether we are conscious of it or not. Our stories are just as powerful to us as adults as they were as children, we are just less aware of them. As we grow up, becoming educated through a system of prescribed learning, we are taught to value the logical, the objective, and that which can be clearly measured and assessed. But in the deep recesses of our animalistic brains, story lurks, informing our thinking in a way that most of us are completely oblivious to.

Stories can be a great ally in helping us to solve our social and environmental woes, provided we use them appropriately. Hearing stories can release brain chemicals such as oxytocin and cortisol, evoking an empathy response and even inspiring post-story actions such as making a donation.[1] The story in my poem of the woman walking many miles down a dusty road to gather water was one that encouraged the audience to reflect on how lucky many of us are to have the convenience of clean, fresh water at the turn of a tap. And yet, stories have their limitations. Usually with a beginning, middle, and end, and a limited set of characters, they do not always encourage us to think systemically. The story of one individual, group, or community often tells us little about the wider context of everything else going on. While we might feel sympathy for the woman who has to walk for miles every day, hearing about her experience tells us nothing about the political situation that might be limiting her access to fresh water. It doesn't tell us about the cultural importance that might be placed upon this role. It doesn't tell us whether or not her husband thanks her for her labour at the end of a long day, or whether she also experiences joy and meaning in her life. In short, the story is narrow and incomplete. No stories are completely objective, and nor do they tell the whole story. The person or organisation telling a story will always have some subjective lens they are looking through. Our societies also tend to value some stories over others, depending on who is telling the story and their position within a culture. Factors such as race, age, gender, religion, education, and social standing influence whose stories are elevated, celebrated, and retold, and whose are not. To understand the problems that we are facing as a global society, we need to start treating everyone's stories as equally important, and to recognise that there are many factors influencing any given story.

———

Narratives are a system or collection of related stories that are inherently felt or understood to be true. They are the lenses and filters through which we see the world, mental models that serve as collective proxies for "the way things are." They are non-linear and messy, and are heavily influenced by culture, upbringing, tradition, creed, and values. Because of this, narratives are generally collectively built and inherited, passed down through social norms, memories, anecdotes, songs, myths, and legends, and other cultural practices.

While stories are told, narratives are more felt and understood at a gut level. Shortly before Christmas in 2012, a monumental display of human generosity and kindness played out in a Tim Hortons coffee and doughnut drive-through in Winnipeg, Canada. One kind customer kicked it off by paying for the order of the car behind them in the drive-through queue. The customer in the following car then followed suit, paying for the order behind them. Over the course of three hours, 228 customers participated in this chain of paying-it-forward for whichever stranger happened to be in the car behind them.

Through each person's simple yet powerful act of kindness, the social narrative that everyone is out for themselves was torn down for a few hours and replaced with something a little more beautiful. The "rational actor" assumption that people weigh up the costs and benefits of every decision to assess what will be best for them alone is one that underpins our modern economy and society. Yet on this particular day, these strangers collectively rejected that assumption. Rather, each of those 228 customers may share the story long into the future, of that one time in the Tim Hortons drive-through when they broke the rules of capitalism in a small yet powerful way.

I believe many of our unexamined narratives are doing us a lot of harm as a global society. The narrative that technology will solve all our problems means that we ignore the social reality that only some of us will have access to those technologies. The narrative that tells us that the gifts of nature are ours for the taking is destroying ecosystems across the world. The narrative that industrial-scale, monocultural agriculture is the only way to feed a growing global population is destroying our soils and polluting our waterways. The narratives of meritocracy and free market economics tell us that the rich are deserving and the poor equally so. These narratives persist, despite a growing awareness around the influences of human bias, systemic discrimination, geopolitical inequities, and the fact that those who have money in the first place can more easily increase their wealth exponentially. While they may hold a lot of sway, and are in some cases perpetuated by those who seek to retain power and wealth, they are not narratives that are supportive of a thriving global population living harmoniously within the confines of a limited biosphere.

The interplay between narrative and the way we conduct our lives is symbiotic. In crude terms, human beings are basically pack animals who seek belonging by behaving in ways that are consistent with the norms, cultures, and unspoken agreements of any given group, community, or society. That is, we largely adhere to the narratives that tell us how to be "normal." Even in counter cultures, there are in-group narratives that inform how to behave. A person who considers themselves a goth cannot one day decide to wear a sequin-spangled pair of rainbow hot pants without risking raising the eyebrows of other goths. A high-powered CEO is not going to suggest that the company holds its next board meeting at the local food court to save on expenses. The narratives we hold inform our day-to-day actions, just as our everyday actions and identities inform what we hold to be true.

By putting myself through a month of extreme water conservation and writing "The Water Poem," I challenged the predominantly Western narrative of water as a limitless, instant resource that flows freely at the turn of a tap. It was an uphill battle in some regards. Many people couldn't understand how my stunt could make a difference. I received my fair share of trolls on media articles about my experience who questioned my motivations ("Some people will do anything for 15 minutes of fame!") and personal hygiene ("Gross, imagine how she smells!"). It is impossible for any one of us to enact narrative change alone. But just as tiny tugboats can make subtle shifts in the direction of a giant hulking ocean liner, the stories and frames that we use on a daily basis in both our work and personal lives can slowly shift mainstream narratives over time. Once the ship is moving, it's incredible how fast alternative narratives can spread when enough people start paying attention to new norms. Following World War II, the narratives surrounding women's roles in the workplace changed radically after it had become necessary for women to work in factories and shipyards while the men were away at war. We saw such seismic shifts during the Renaissance, when the value of the intellect became a guiding narrative. When New Zealand banned single-use plastic bags in 2019, supermarkets phased them out six months earlier than they were legally required to —such was the pressure from the public who had come to accept a new narrative about the environmental cost of convenience. Eighteen months later, the government put forth a proposal to phase out seven other types of single-use plastics including plastic straws, cutlery, sushi trays, and polystyrene packaging. Even five years earlier this would have seemed unimaginable. At a collective scale, narrative change is culture change. While many of these narrative shifts have historically been emergent in nature, practices such as narrative foresight can help us to be more intentional by crafting stories of preferable futures.[2] Rather than forecasting the future, which is a practice that relies heavily on the influence of the past and present, we can imagine what we want it to look like and then work backwards to figure out how we get there.

A certain type of narrative warrants mention here, the kind that is so ubiquitous it is almost universal in its control over our lives. *Meta narratives* or *deep narratives* are the sorts of global assumptions about how the world works that have so infiltrated our psyche that they are widely held to be true, the whole world over. They are often unquestionable without risking sounding like a raving lunatic, completely disconnected from reality. Examples of meta narratives include the idea that we need money to live; that we need to organise different populations into countries with clear geopolitical borders; or that people whose jobs create profit for shareholders deserve to be paid more than people who work to improve their communities and create non-financial forms of value. Arguing against these narratives may not always win you many friends, but it is worth remembering that they are socially constructed realities. Money and borders are not functions of the natural world. For many decades, vested interests have been lobbying governments and spending billions of dollars in social marketing to embed narratives that support their business or agenda. The only reason we pay more to corporate executives than nurses and environmental rights advocates is that our societies, governing systems, and cultures have collectively come to value the creation of economic wealth over healthy lives and clean environments. If we are to truly shift the systems upon which our world is built, and drive transformational change, we need to be prepared to closely examine our most universally held narratives.

One particularly interesting experiment that has emerged over the past decade to counter predominant economic meta narratives is Free Money Day. Held each year since 2011 on September 15—the anniversary of the day that Lehman Brothers filed for bankruptcy during the Global Financial Crisis—the event encourages people to give money to strangers with a request that they pass along half of it to someone else. By removing the transactional association with money, and instead embedding a relational model of gifting, it encourages people to think about the value, purpose, and culture of money that by and large we accept without questioning. In short, it encourages us to examine the narratives that we hold about money.

———

Long ago, before the internet, before computers, before books, there was myth. The carrying system for lesson delivery, myths are symbolic stories or narratives that highlight a collective truth. No matter how the predominant norms of the day might change, myths are the timeless anchors to our common humanity. They often take on a spiritual quality, holding up a mirror and exposing our deepest truths. From the moment of birth, we carry many myths on our tiny shoulders. They speak to what is happening inside us, reassuring us of who we are, where we have come from, and our place in life as we navigate the outer world. Myths represent the whimsical, the magical, the fable, the legend. Originally born out of a need to explain natural phenomena in the absence of scientific understanding, myths were created by early humans to make sense of the world around them. Traditionally, they were handed down orally from person to person, generation to generation, translating and transferring the cultural values of our ancestors. For example, the myth of the lost city of Atlantis, which originated from Greek philosopher Plato, told of an advanced utopian civilisation that eventually became greedy and immoral. Consequently, the city was destroyed by the gods. The lesson communicated within this myth is to be careful not to let greed take over and to live a good and moral life.

Myths don't profess to be literal truths. They rather contain a seed of truth wrapped up in story, and therein lies their universal appeal. Yet, in the Western world, which values science and rationality, many of us tend not to place much value on that which cannot be empirically proven. Such has been our emphasis on rational thought that the word *myth* itself has come to be culturally synonymous with "lies," "falsehood," or "a story or theory that is not true." From that which was once revered, transcendent, supernatural even, myth has become less of a force that inspires and guides people and cultures, and more akin to a weapon wielded by those who seek to discredit another's point of view. We hear phrases like "climate change is a myth" or "trickle-down economics is a myth," suggesting that these things are farcical or untrue.

Compounding our neglect of myth as a central guiding force in our lives, observance and practice of religion is on the decline around the world. While the elevation of science has provided great leaps forward in medicine, agriculture, technology, and urban planning, the loss of adherence to something more mysterious, something greater than ourselves, and greater than the sum of its parts has many of us searching for deeper meaning. I know it certainly has for me. I find it somewhat ironic that despite science telling us that we have so much yet to learn about the human brain, we still have unwavering faith in the power of our intellect above the other psychological functions like sensing, feeling, and intuiting. These were highlighted in popular culture by psychologist Carl Jung but have also been embedded within the traditional knowledge systems of indigenous cultures around the world for countless generations.

One of the most significant myths to fall by the wayside in our modern lives is the one that says we are intricately connected with each other and with the natural world. Putting aside the biophysical truth to this idea—we after all exchange 98 percent of the atoms in our bodies with the world around us every year—this story that we are separate from each other and from nature is a convenient one. It is much easier for us to excuse our exploitation of the environment if we consider ourselves separate from it. It is much easier to trample upon the rights of other people if we consider ourselves discrete individuals rather than a collective species. In the Māori language, there is an oft-quoted whakataukī (proverb) that says "Ko au te awa, ko te awa ko au," which translates to "I am the river, the river is me." While it is symbolic to most of us, many Māori understand this mythology as literal. As the Indigenous people of New Zealand, ancestry is traced back not only to people but also to the mountains and rivers that nurtured their ancestors. It is a story that science and Western rational thought tells us is not true. But in part I think it is the casual casting aside of such a mythic narrative that enables us to collectively do so much harm to our home planet.

Fellow spoken word artist Sharn Maree is working actively to spread narratives of connection, using her voice to weave the mythological with the modern. With a quiet confidence and commanding stage presence, she skilfully blends strategic framing, storytelling, narrative, and myth to shine light on systemic problems:

 Storytelling has the ability to tell the ugly but make it beautiful. People are more receptive to hearing the ugly truth when it's wrapped up in a bow. It's sad, but it's true, right? It makes them feel better about it. So that's how poetic stories with beautiful language can help if we want to reunite societal mindsets with the importance of respecting Papatūānuku (Mother Earth), and acknowledging that we're only here as temporary guardians for the next generation.

Sharn is Māori of Ngāpuhi and Te-Whānau-ā-Apanui descent, iwi (extended kinship groups, similar to a band, nation, or tribe) from the Far North and East Coast regions of the North Island, and is also of Irish and Welsh ancestry. Her poetry covers the challenges of navigating life as wahine Māori (a Māori woman) in a society that she has found intent on putting her in a box. As a former youth worker, she has seen a lot of angles to the social challenges that New Zealand is facing. Sharn's poems cover themes such as mental health, New Zealand's shocking rates of child abuse and child poverty, and the disproportionate levels of Māori incarceration in the country's prisons. She possesses the knack of raising these heavy issues in an incredibly powerful, yet graceful and inviting way:

> I want to start conversations and stir people's minds about things that have been sitting right in front of them that they maybe haven't acknowledged, or that they may have acknowledged and then just moved on—societal misgivings, mental health, and the mindset of society as a whole. The mindset that tells us we need to 'stick to our side of the fence' as opposed to reaching out to support others. The mindset that sees us blaming governments or policy, and not acknowledging how we as individuals contribute towards these systems that perpetuate the issues we face today. How do we heal when partnership has been spoken to rather than with, participation is invite only, and protection is a concrete cage? The healing is in our stories— through sharing them, we have the power to heal ourselves and others as well. It's a superpower, using your words.

More recently, Sharn worked in a government department helping to publish the stories of treaty settlements in Aotearoa —the Māori name for New Zealand. These are financial settlements between the Crown and individual iwi, to compensate for historical theft of land, loss of economic livelihoods, and other devastating Crown breaches of New Zealand's founding document, te Tiriti o Waitangi (the Treaty of Waitangi). She admits that government is a frustrating place to change predominant narratives, given its slow-moving nature, but she has a trust in the emergence of new stories through repetition. Sharn is under no illusions that we'll see full agreement across society as to what our narratives of the future should be but stresses that what is more important is Māori stories being told by Māori, and an openness to hearing each other's stories. Sharn says:

> Māori have a whakataukī, 'He aha te kai a te Rangatira? He kōrero, he kōrero, he kōrero.' What is the food of the leader? It is knowledge, it is communication. We are a culture that largely passed down our traditional practices and history orally. It is an important part of our being to share these stories so that our next generation can learn who they are and where they come from; so that future generations don't grow up lost without a sense of identity. I guess it's about just getting the ball rolling, encouraging people, and creating safe spaces for people to explore the real history of Aotearoa, not the watered-down version.

Sharn comes from a long line of orators and a culture of storytelling, and her journey into spoken word has been supported by a deepening of her relationship with te ao Māori (the Māori worldview). It was a culture unknown to her as a child and she got a government loan in her mid-thirties in order to study the language and reclaim that part of her heritage. She recently received a moko kauae—a facial tattoo covering the chin that is traditionally carried by Māori women as an outward expression of whakapapa (genealogy). On how her poetry has developed, Sharn says:

> Storytelling is just what our people do, it's how we pass on our sacred ways and our mātauranga, our knowledge. So I take great pride and a sense of comfort in that. But the more I've gotten to know

my culture and revitalise my relationship with it, the better my writing has become and the easier the words have flowed. It's like I've turned on a tap.

Indigenous narratives around collectivism and connection to the world around us are increasingly influencing other sectors of society. Deep down, I think many of us sense that we are disconnected from each other, from community, and from nature, and from the food that sustains us—the last of which has long been the most tangible link between humans and the natural world. With that realisation comes a sense of loss, grief, loneliness, and anxiety. As a species that has spent the vast majority of our existence in small, close-knit groups of people sustained by our immediate environment, the manner in which many of us now live— especially in large cities—is really quite unnatural. In many ways, it does not recognise the interconnected systems within which we all exist.

3

THE SYSTEMS UNDERPINNING OUR LIVES

THERE'S A SCENE IN THE HBO SHOW *SILICON VALLEY* THAT parodies a large-scale tech conference. As each guy (and it's always a guy) takes the stage to present their latest tech solution, they all announce how they are "making the world a better place" through a range of obscure high-tech products and software services. As with any half-decent parody, the meme is firmly grounded in reality, with the frame of changing the world being hugely popular in the real Silicon Valley and beyond. Leaving aside the irony that many Silicon Valley tech companies are doing little beyond finding ways to make life marginally more streamlined or entertaining for a privileged few, the pursuit of purpose within business is gaining significant traction. The rise of social enterprise and impact entrepreneurship presents those who want to create change with the opportunity to embed social or environmental change at the very core of their company's purpose. In the UK alone, social enterprise contributed £ 60 billion to the economy in 2019—representing a little over 2 percent of the country's GDP.[1] Within large companies, Corporate Social Responsibility (CSR) provides an avenue for companies to engage in fair trade, ethical employment practices, philanthropic activities, and charitable work. Third party accreditation systems such as B Corporations provide assurance to customers that companies are meeting certain environmental and social performance criteria. These mechanisms are a great starting point. But they are limited in what they can achieve in that they often only address change on the explicit level, leaving many of the underlying root causes of our problems unchallenged.

Since the dawn of the Industrial Age, there has been a workplace trend towards specialisation in one particular area of knowledge. There is a distinct economic advantage for those who know more about one narrow area of focus than their competitors. This has been a great boon for productivity, but it has split the world up into silos. With a deep knowledge of only one part of an interconnected system, we start to view the world as a collection of distinct and discrete elements that can be manipulated with little or no effect on the others. This is, of course, the polar opposite to the way that the natural world operates. Early systems thinker Donella Meadows once said:

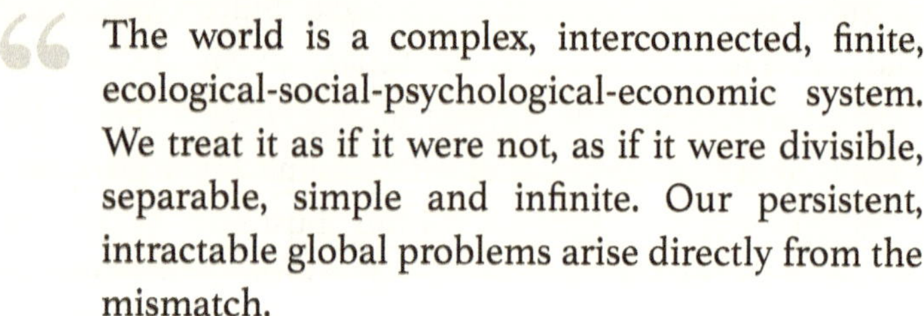

> The world is a complex, interconnected, finite, ecological-social-psychological-economic system. We treat it as if it were not, as if it were divisible, separable, simple and infinite. Our persistent, intractable global problems arise directly from the mismatch.

By splitting the world up into its constituent parts and manipulating those parts in isolation, we ignore the relationships, processes, and interdependencies between them. The world is built up of intricate systems. Natural systems and human-built systems, physical systems, and psychological systems. Nothing exists in a vacuum, and everything exists in the context of everything else. It seems an obvious thing to point out, but when it comes to the work of solving problems that affect humans, other life, and the planet we call home, we are not that great at recognising the systems within which a challenge exists. Systems are intangible, and we often can't see them. Consequently, we do not always properly diagnose issues to understand the scope of the problem. We treat the symptoms, not the cause. The nature of our busy lives is to focus on what is in front of us and to get on with the job, solving problems quickly with the limited resources available to us. We find easy targets to blame in our quest for a simple, linear understanding about how a problem came about and who is responsible. In our rush towards developing solutions for the myriad problems that we face, our lack of appreciation for the wider systems within which a problem exists can lead to ineffectual solutions at best, or actually exacerbating harm at worst. Millions of dollars are thrown at international aid programmes, without an understanding of the cultural contexts within which a community or country experiences hardships. Gig economy technologies within transport and food delivery services are touted as flexible worker-friendly ways to make extra cash on the side, but leave unquestioned the underlying reasons why so many people need to work two or three jobs to stay afloat. We throw education intervention at marginalised young people and encourage them to enter into qualification programmes without understanding the socio-economic, health, and cultural factors that influence their ability to learn within the structural limitations of those programmes. We invest in planting tree monocultures to sequester carbon, and then clear cut them in ways that destroy the carbon sequestering capacity of the soil in which they grow.

Generalists tend to have a bad name when it comes to the workforce, but in this day and age when converging challenges are piling up, we need them more than ever. We need to get away from what Aldous Huxley called "the celibacy of the intellect" and take multi-faceted approaches with diverse viewpoints around the table. To address complex social, environmental, and economic problems such as climate change, rising inequality, systemic racism, political polarisation, and the destruction of our home planet, we need to recognise the multitude of factors at play. We need to consider the many stakeholders involved, the insights that they bring, the assumptions and biases that they equally bring, and the interconnections between all the moving parts of a big, messy tangle of a system. These factors are seldom taken into consideration when a bright young entrepreneur stands up on a stage and suggests that their singular product or idea is going to change the world. Don't get me wrong, the efforts of many social and impact-driven entrepreneurs are laudable. They are a critical piece of the puzzle and are undoubtedly making a difference. Some are indeed already taking a systems approach to their work. Others, however, are building their solutions upon the foundations of broken systems of oppression and inequity. Without widespread cultural, relational, and psychological shifts, many of these efforts are ultimately little more than a Band-Aid when it comes to really shifting the systems that underpin our lives. To solve our most ingrained and complex of problems, we require nothing less than the complete transformation of how humanity lives on this planet and the story of why we are here. And that will need a drastically different approach from the ones we've predominantly been taking so far.

Our systems have been collectively built, and to change them we need to work collectively at three different levels. The first is the *structural* or *institutional* level, which represents policies, practices, and resource flows. The second level is *relational*, concerning our relationships and connections, and the power dynamics between them. Thirdly, the *transformative* level is where we shift mental models of thought, assumptions, and deeply held beliefs.[2] To date, a disproportionate share of the funding, attention, and brain power that is required to address systemic problems has been directed towards the first level. We've made impact-focused *structural* changes to business models and government policies, and through philanthropic or charitable giving. Given that this is where results are most tangible and measurable, and we see a time-bound return on investment, it is not surprising that we have focused here first. It is the low-hanging fruit of systems change. But it is primarily the second and third level that I'll be addressing in this book. At the *relational* level, the strategic use of storytelling can heal our relationships with each other and our home planet, and help to reconfigure the skewed power dynamics that contribute to social and environmental problems. This in turn helps to change systems on the *transformational* level, as we see shifts in the broad underlying narratives that we hold to be true about life, society, and our place within it. From there, we also see feedback loops to increased *structural* change as the cultural capacity to envisage and believe in a better future drives the political will to make it so.

———

It is a strange paradox that in one sense we are more connected than ever through digital means, yet that same instant connection has also served to divide us. Since the advent of the internet, twenty-four-hour news cycles, and social media, we are able to learn on a daily basis what is going on halfway around the world. These tools should be opening our eyes to different points of view and helping us to understand more about the world and its systems. But instead, they have come to serve as agents of division and distancing. The great promise of the internet, to democratise access to knowledge and provide for the advancement of humankind, has been derailed by algorithmic shenanigans that only show us what we like, and a widespread call-out culture that reinforces our own viewpoints and has made us intolerant of people who think differently.

Prior to the Information Age, the goings-on of other countries were of little consequence. We might have read about them in the World section of our morning newspaper, but whatever was happening many thousands of miles from us had little bearing on our immediate lives and daily situations. For many of us, it still doesn't. The deforestation of the Amazon is far from our minds, even as we directly experience increasingly erratic weather patterns and natural disasters thanks in part due to the removal of such massive carbon sinks from the biosphere. Many of us don't carefully dissect how our daily consumption, transport, and dietary choices affect the rest of the planet and the other people on it. While twenty-four-hour news from around the globe has helped us to know what is going on, it has also had a numbing effect. The problems are too large and the systems too complex for us to wrap our heads around. The media tend to favour coverage of the negative, providing a skewed lens on the overall state of things. It is tempting to take a fatalistic view of our current state and future trajectory. How can we, each of us a minuscule part of a giant, overwhelming system, possibly hope to enact change? The silver lining lies in recognising that the systems we are operating within were built by people. The functioning of all anthropological systems is not beholden to the laws of the physical world, but is rather underpinned by our narratives, assumptions, and norms. As Carl Jung said:

> The gigantic catastrophes that threaten us today are not elemental happenings of a physical or biological order, but psychic events. To a quite terrifying degree we are threatened by wars and revolutions which are nothing other than psychic epidemics. At any moment several million human beings may be smitten with a new madness, and then we shall have another world war or devastating revolution. Instead of being at the mercy of wild beasts, earthquakes, landslides, and inundations, modern man is battered by the elemental forces of his own psyche.

Because it was us who created the systems that have birthed our biggest challenges, it is us who can change them. And just as these systems have been collectively built, the work of changing them must be collectively undertaken. When the United Nations' Millennium Development Goals expired in 2015, they were replaced by a set of new goals. The Sustainable Development Goals (SDGs) expanded on the prior mandate to tackle poverty, hunger, disease, and a lack of education in less well-off countries, to include goals focused on a healthy, thriving natural world. This widening of scope sent a signal to the world that the problems we are facing are not confined to the countries that we usually frame as "less developed," but that the goals are relevant to us all, and that achieving them is going to take a global effort. The inclusion of environmentally focused goals also serves to recognise that progress towards the goals needs to take a systemic approach. All of these efforts need to happen in tandem. We cannot eliminate poverty and hunger without addressing climate change and its devastating role in driving drought and widespread crop failures. We cannot have clean water and sanitation without respecting the lifeforms that live within rivers and lakes and the roles they play in the healthy functioning of freshwater ecosystems. And we cannot solve environmental challenges without solving the social issues required to get everybody on board. All are interconnected. All are intertwined. We do not solve problems by simply fixing the thing that we see as the problem; we solve them by closely examining, rebuilding, or replacing the problematic systems from which they have arisen. When it comes down to it, each of our biggest social and environmental challenges is a cultural challenge—it is our perceptions of these problems that are the biggest challenges to overcome.

For a brief moment in 1968, the world saw the whole Earth as a system. The images taken on the Apollo 8 mission presented a powerful piece of visual storytelling unveiling our home planet for what it really is: a delicate, vibrant, tiny blue and green sphere floating amid the vast nothingness of space. Suddenly humanity was not a collection of countries and opponents, but a single species living on an ephemeral ball of life. The images had a profound effect on us, birthing the modern environmental movement and sowing the seeds of a new narrative of humankind as a collective. Since 1968, however, we have strayed much more into narratives of individualism over collectivism. Modern-day capitalism, a real and perceived scarcity of resources, increasing polarisation, and the ways in which we structure our homes and communities have nurtured a culture where it is normal and acceptable to look out only for yourself and your nearest and dearest. A culture where it is quite usual to sit down on a bus or plane next to someone for an hour or twelve and never utter a word to each other. Our recent ancestors, even of a century or two ago, would have considered this kind of behaviour bizarre and anti-social. When it comes down to it, it is; humans evolved in small groups dependent upon each other for survival: individualism is inherently anti-social. The norm of individualism in many

Western cultures supports our impulse to deal with problems discretely—we'll deal with our own problems, thank you very much, we don't need the help of others. The global wellness market, valued in 2018 at US$4.5 trillion,[3] focuses almost entirely on health and wellness as individual choice. This approach to healthcare undermines the responsibility of countries to fix the conditions under which so many people are not doing well. It leaves unquestioned the collective upstream factors such as working conditions, healthcare policy, food regulation, poverty, transport planning, and access to mental health services, all of which contribute to an individual's wellness. The prevailing narrative of the wellness industry also inherently suggests that if a person is unwell, it is their own fault because they didn't sufficiently take care of themselves, instead of taking into account all those other contributing factors.

It is difficult to tell the stories surrounding problems in the context of wider systems precisely because they are so complex. Human minds love a simple story. We gravitate towards simplistic linear plots, with goodies and baddies, and a beginning, middle, and end. But this kind of storytelling is not always appropriate for addressing the complexity of the problems we face on this planet. With only a narrow thread of the story, we risk drawing conclusions and attempting to make sense of things with incomplete information. The importance of how we frame stories to support systems change is highlighted in Shanto Iyengar's 1991 book, *Is Anyone Responsible? How Television Frames Political Issues*. He introduced the concepts of episodic and thematic framing in reference to how the news media tells stories. Episodic stories, which draw heavily on case studies or events, are framed to focus on individuals rather than issues. They tell the isolated story of a single event or episode, without mentioning the external conditions or circumstances in which the event occurred. No context is given around trends over time, prior happenings leading up to the episode, or the socio-political landscape that supported or influenced the event to unfold the way it did. Iyengar found that when exposed to this kind of framing in television news reports, people were more likely to attribute the source and responsibility of a problem to the individual(s) involved, rather than the system within which they are embedded. In the absence of contextual information, the audience draws on their own biases, experiences, and beliefs to fill the gaps. Thematic framing on the other hand aims to introduce context, nesting the story within the wider environment. It makes use of multiple rather than singular examples, probes related issues, references historical trends and policies, and generally investigates the *why* of a story rather than just the *who*, *what*, and *how*. Viewers exposed to thematic framing are more likely to view the problems as public ones, and see government and other civic organisations as responsible for fixing them rather than the individuals involved. The murder of George Floyd in mid-2020 by Minneapolis police officer Derek Chauvin could have resulted in yet another episodic story about a black man dying after a scuffle with the law. But instead, thanks to the prior work of the Black Lives Matter movement, countless historical pioneers, and the added pressure of outrage from many new sectors of society, some news outlets began talking more seriously about the systemic issues at play. The story became thematic as statistics were introduced into the conversation about the prevalence of killing of black men at the hands of police officers, and as other factors were discussed relating to systemic racism, poverty, and marginalisation of black communities. The footage of Chauvin kneeling on Floyd's neck for almost ten minutes, captured thanks to the bravery and quick thinking of 17-year-old Darnella Frazier, makes for harrowing viewing. The casual nonchalance shown by police officers once Floyd had lost consciousness points to a systemic or routine lack of care, and the footage proved to be pivotal in the jury reaching a guilty verdict.

The worldwide spread of support for Black Lives Matter during 2020 also demonstrates the process of emergence. The weight of this movement did not arise from the murder of George Floyd. It did not begin with Eric Garner or Michael Brown, two others who had earlier died at the hands of police. It did not even begin with the acquittal of George Zimmerman after he shot unarmed teenager Trayvon Martin, although that's when the social media hashtag #BlackLivesMatter began to appear. Within the US, it began years, decades, centuries before, dating back to before the Civil War, with the early efforts of slavery abolitionists. Each step of these prior movements built upon the last, like sun drying the kindling, ready for the spark to take flame when the moment emerged when the story couldn't help but change. The previous loss of black lives at the hands of the police, rooted in the legacy of slavery and a culture of white supremacy, paved the way for this simple yet effective narrative to spread across the world—the narrative that black lives do indeed matter. In the psyche of a great swath of the public, the value of black lives ceased to be "a black issue" in 2020, and instead became one of a deeply flawed and unjust system in which we are all a part.

When we look to how change happens in nature, short of a natural disaster or some grand Earth-shattering event, the changes are never the result of top-down strategies or of preconceived ideas of how things are going to change. There is no grand plan with buy-in from all the moving parts of an impossibly intricate natural system. The changes begin at a localised level, perhaps happening simultaneously in many small, yet geographically disconnected areas. From the outside, it may appear as if nothing much is happening. But over time, all of these hundreds and thousands of small actions or localised elements of change become connected and suddenly add up to something hugely powerful. Structural change within human-built systems happens in a similar way. Policies and politicians have a role to play, but the true power lies with the strength of diverse and distributed groups and individuals whose collective efforts are greater than the sum of their parts. Separate groups of people may converge around a shared issue, with each group comprising members with different skill sets, passions, experiences, histories, and interests in the problem. As these networks grow and begin to talk to each other, we start to see the emergence of new systems and cross-pollination of thinking. Or it might happen much more organically with similar conclusions being reached by many groups without coordinated cooperation of efforts. Whatever the process of emergence, it is the stories and coherent shared narratives that serve as guiding stars showing us the way.

Just as no single ingredient in a cake can tell you what the end result will taste like, the power in emergent networks and movements cannot be judged by the individuals and groups that support them. Each influences the other, and collectively they come up with ideas or solutions that no one would have guessed would be possible when they began working together. A great example of emergent culture within the workplace is that of Enspiral, an international collaborative network of entrepreneurs, freelancers, software developers, designers, artists, activists, systems thinkers, and other professionals who are united in their desire to work on social impact, or in their words, "stuff that matters." Emerging in 2010 in New Zealand's capital city, Wellington, the original handful of people involved helped each other to find work that aligned with their vision of a world that was more equitable and just. In turn they pooled a proportion of their income together to pay for minimal administrative costs and office rental. When the network needed new tools or services, people would get their heads together and new ventures would pop up to provide the scaffolding. Everything was open source, so that it could be replicated by other similar groups around the world. When I learned of Enspiral in 2012, it looked from the outside to be an amazing, albeit moderately intimidating tight-knit group of really talented and dedicated people who had somehow magically built this well-oiled model of working collaboratively, despite their wildly diverse skill sets and interests. When I joined in late 2013, I was amazed at how little was predetermined or planned out in detail. Anyone in the network could suggest ideas or changes, and decisions were made collectively. It was completely non-hierarchical, there was no central plan, and the people involved were very much building the ship as they journeyed together.

While the network is constantly evolving with about 150 contributors spread across eighteen countries, and many additional friends and collaborators, the core ethos remains the same today. Around thirty core members who make key decisions are supported by a "minimum viable board." Cross-pollination with other similar networks who value open source, cooperative methods of working, and non-hierarchical organisational structures, has strengthened both Enspiral and other communities of practice. The decentralised network challenges the organisational narratives that hierarchical structures are needed to get things done; that products, processes, and services should be proprietary; that maximising profits is the purpose of business; and that the competition is to be quashed at all costs. Enspiral works because the people involved believe in a simple vision: regardless of what we do, it's better when we work together. Just as natural ecosystems are at their most robust with an abundance of biodiversity, human systems thrive with a diversity of talents, ideas, gifts and contributions.

4

HUMANITY AT THE CROSSROADS

IT'S ONE THING TO BUY A COUPLE OF COFFEES FOR THE PERSON behind you in the drive-through, but what about paying off someone's student loan? In the middle of the 2020 northern hemisphere summer, as the United States was struggling to get COVID-19 under control and Black Lives Matter was receiving worldwide media attention, this is exactly what happened to Sonya Renee Taylor. Sonya is an author, poet, speaker, and activist best known for her work founding The Body Is Not an Apology—a website, *New York Times* bestselling book, and movement aimed at fostering radical self-love and the acceptance of all bodies. Going far beyond the usual ideas of body positivity, Sonya's core theory of change is that we cannot transform the world around us until we transform our relationships with ourselves, our bodies, and the bodies of others in all their shapes, sizes, colours, ages, sexualities, and levels of ability. I first met Sonya at a poetry slam in San Francisco in 2012, where I was blown away by her presence and power with words. In recent years, Sonya has built a large following on social media with her raw, vulnerable videos that unpack racial oppression and other social justice issues in a graceful, eloquent, and yet unapologetic way, and challenge people to examine their own stories and narratives closely.

As Black Lives Matter was picking up steam, she floated the idea in one of her Instagram videos of some sort of initiative to buy back black debt in the United States—debt that she sees as largely incurred by black people through the mere act of participation in an unjust society underpinned by systemic racism. When we spoke via video call, she explained the thinking behind the idea:

 I thought of this idea around how to begin the repair of relationships between black folks and white folks at the intersection of spiritual and material debt. It was basically about getting people with wealth to pay off the systemic, inequitable debt that black people owe, particularly the debt that is a function of the state or institutions, so student loans, mortgages, taxes, those sorts of things. It's recognising that all kinds of debt are institutional in some way, and I see this as a tool and structure to do transformational interracial healing work.

When Sonya refers to institutional debt, she's talking about the systemic issues at play, both historical and current, that mean black people need to take on debt more readily than white people. She's highlighting the intergenerational transfer of white wealth that not so long ago was earned on the backs of black people through slave labour. She's referring to black folks who were arrested for petty crimes in their twenties and couldn't afford a lawyer, so they took a plea deal and spent mandatory minimum sentences in privatised prisons that turned a profit at their expense. She's referring to the systemic racism that means employers may be less likely to take on black employees, pay them less if they do, and fire them more readily for minor infractions.

By buying back that black debt, Sonya sees a tangible way to reorient the toxic narrative of black poverty from one of laziness or inherent badness to one of systemic oppression:

> There is power in closing the wealth gap, because these are the kinds of things that keep black people from attaining economic parity. We can clearly connect wealth to privilege, opportunity, and resource. It's not to say that white folks' wealth has come absent of hard work. But there is a difference between hard work that meets opportunity versus hard work meeting systemic racism.

The idea snowballed, and not long after she launched the campaign, an Instagram follower named Brenda Barros Rivera offered to organise a fundraising drive to pay off Sonya's US$114,000 student loan. Another follower, Kaitlin May, offered to accept and redirect international payments. Within three and a half weeks, the loan was paid off in full, with almost six thousand dollars overpaid. Both Brenda and Kaitlin were unknown to Sonya, but through her vulnerable, heartfelt stories and challenging truths shared on social media, she has built a community based on integrity and trust. Some 200 people outside the US re-routed international payments through Kaitlin, putting their trust in a complete stranger to do what she said she would with the money. Sonya believes this leap of faith they took was thanks to a belief in the vision and the sense of disrupting prevailing narratives surrounding black debt, along with narratives we hold about the purpose of money. It was something tangible that people could do, not so much out of a sense of white guilt, but out of a genuine recognition that they had inadvertently benefited from the systemic oppression of black folks:

> Money is just an exchange of energy; we can use that energy as a sign of our lack and our fears, or it can be the energy of love. The only reason we hoard money is that we associate it with a sense of lack. What if we didn't value money? If giving money was as genuine an expression as smiling at a stranger, or holding a dying person's hand, then of course we would just give it as freely as we give smiles. That's the economic system I want to live in … I feel like a thousand people reached out and said, 'I'll hold your hand.'

The paying off of Sonya's debt runs counter to predominant narratives around rational self-interest, individualism, poverty and the reasons people become trapped in it, and equality of opportunity. By dismantling those narratives for one person, those people were able to peel away the layers of these narratives and start participating in a new story:

> It's been so beautiful to watch. People have told me about how the act of giving was transformative for them, how they felt like they were part of some much larger thing. All of a sudden, it's a whole group of people who do not know each other, but are all contributing to this one vision and getting a chance to see that vision come into being. Everybody deserves to have the chance to have the impossible be made possible. I think a huge part of the reason why systems don't change is because

people just don't believe it's possible to change them. But this is how we interrupt institutional inequity and economic racism in a very practical, clear, and transformative way.

Of course, this model does not address the fundamental reasons many black folks need to take on debt in the first place. On an individual level, it is a Band-Aid. But the real power is at the collective level. What it does achieve is to encourage people to closely question and understand the systemic issues at play. Sonya hopes that by highlighting one of the problems associated with systemic racism and offering a tangible solution for people to counter the effects one person at a time, we can start to slowly shift narratives:

 We exist in a worldwide experience of contagion right now, because we are interdependent. So in a period of contagion, the question becomes, What is it that we want to spread? We humans don't only spread bad things. We can spread joy, we can spread wealth. The question is, What will we be intentional about spreading?

———

On March 1, 2020, I sat down at my desk with an air of conviction and determination, as I began what was to be a three-month period of intensive writing to get this book out of my head and onto the page. Twenty-six days later, New Zealand went into full COVID-19 lockdown, and out the window went my resolve and optimism, along with much of what I assumed to be true about my comfortable life in Wellington. The novel coronavirus that began its clean sweep of the globe in early 2020 was a jolt to our sense of normality, and presented a shake-up to many of the narratives underpinning our lives. The reality of global interdependence came crashing home, as we realised the utter inadequacy of a national border to stop a virus. The idea of shutting down international air travel across the globe, which just a few months prior was an impossible thought, suddenly held truth. The first major global pandemic since the Asian flu of 1957–58, there was an unreal sense of being part of something so large, so widespread, so far beyond the realm of previous comprehension, as billions of people around the world were ordered to stay at home. Notions of control over the natural world were shown to be an illusion, while at the same time, many of us found the lack of traffic noise and sudden proliferation of birdsong and curious wildlife to be a stark reminder of how close nature really is, when we just stop to listen. In many cultures, we saw narratives shifting around the value of collective action, the ways in which we work, and the value of low-wage yet suddenly critical jobs in food distribution, healthcare, and transport.

Forced into a time of pause and reflection, many of us began to question what was really important and to reassess our lives and priorities accordingly. There is nothing like the closure of all the cafes, restaurants, and takeaway outlets and a sudden abundance of time at home to remind you of the beauty and simplicity of a home-cooked meal. There is nothing quite like building a blanket fort with your children on a Tuesday morning to remind you how much you miss the sense of childlike wonder that your busy day-to-day life doesn't make room for. There's nothing like seeing the levelling off of those steeply rising greenhouse gas charts to make you realise just how much agency and potential we humans do actually have to halt the drivers of climate change.

I spent the lockdown tending a tiny garden in the back of our apartment complex in Wellington and playing—really playing

—with my children. I immersed myself in native New Zealand bush up on Wellington's Mount Victoria almost every day. I noticed people walking more slowly than they usually do along the popular trails. On several occasions, I saw them standing still simply taking in the view, admiring a tree, or watching birds play in the twilight. Despite the extreme anxiety I felt about what was happening and the stresses of being stuck at home in a two-bedroom apartment with two energetic preschoolers, I felt myself undergoing a transformation of sorts, facilitated by a slower pace of life and the gradual acceptance of a loss of control over many aspects of my existence. Calls with friends and social commentary all over the internet suggested I wasn't the only one undergoing such a shift in mindset.

As a consequence of this widespread awakening, everything is up for close examination: the story of today's version of capitalism that relies on open international trade routes and exploitative labour practices in far-off lands; the narrative of infinite growth on a finite planet; the idea that we are separate entities whose destinies are solely of our own making; and the cult of productivity at the cost of quality of life. We have realised that what is normal in the context of our everyday modern lives is far from natural. At this very moment, we are occupying a liminal time in the history of our species. We are standing at the threshold of many forthcoming changes, preparing to step into the unknown. But we are not alone. We have the trust of our instincts, we have co-journeyers alongside us, and we have countless generations of ancestors sitting on our shoulders, quietly guiding us if we wish to listen. Not discounting the devastation, the tragedy of people dying alone in isolation, the economic disruption, and the loss of livelihoods for millions that COVID-19 has caused, the virus has also presented us with a unique gift—an opportunity to write a new story of humanity and the way we operate on this planet. We have glimpsed what might be possible in the future if we all work together, and what we do now will matter for many decades and centuries to come. Ultimately, our biggest challenge is in overcoming our assumptions, our biases, and our egos. This is our collective moment of reckoning, but we need not feel chastised. We can instead embrace it as an opportunity for imagination, blue-sky thinking, flexibility, a much deeper sense of connection, and the courage of conviction to return to our values across all levels of society. Humanity has the tools, the technology, the science, and the intellectual know-how to solve virtually all of our great global social and environmental challenges. What we need now is a revolution in human cooperation and genuine connection with those who we have more in common with than we grant ourselves the time to understand. The work of reducing global and local inequality, eliminating racism, transitioning to clean energy, growing healthy food, healing the environment, bringing climate change under control, building regenerative economies, and living happier, healthier lives, requires nothing less than a complete overhaul of the many interconnected systems upon which our lives and societies are built. It's a tall order, but the alternatives are bleak.

To achieve such a magnitude of orchestrated changes, I believe we need to return to the most fundamental driver of human behaviour— the power of story. Humanity currently stands at a crossroads, and what we do over the next ten years or so will define the trajectory of the future for many generations to come. Although we have a monumental task ahead of us that will require widespread combined effort, the more often we tell stories and use language that paints a more beautiful, compassionate, and connected world, the more we can redefine what it means to be human in this liminal moment in time. Author, speaker, and philosopher Charles Eisenstein suggests that humanity has been living in a story of separation, and that we are currently occupying a "space between stories" as we move towards a new (and yet ancient) story of interconnectedness.[1] Systems theorist and deep ecology expert Joanna Macy encourages us to embrace "the great turning," a complete revision of our values and perceptions towards the planet, rather than continuing down the current path of "the great unravelling."[2] British-Sudanese journalist Nesrine Malik writes of six toxic myths that are driving our age of discontent and division, including those surrounding political correctness and perceived attacks on free speech.[3] Campaigner and former UK political adviser Alex Evans calls the disconnect the myth gap,[4] and suggests that to unify humanity and better look after the planet, we need three new myths. The myth of "a larger us" is grounded in the idea that we have more in common than we often believe. The myth of "a longer now" encourages us to start thinking in much longer timeframes. The third myth suggests a better definition of "the good life," in the recognition that endless consumption is not going to fill the hole in our hearts that disconnection has created. I expand on these ideas in Section 4, along with a number of additional new guiding myths for humanity that I think can help us to reorient the defining narratives of our time. The rest of this book is dedicated to uncovering how we can redefine our relationship with language, storytelling, narrative, and authentic listening to give us a decent chance of creating a world that is more regenerative, equitable, just, and full of joy. But first, here's the poem that kicked the journey off for me.

Watch a video of this poem

I haven't had a shower in 28 days
and it's fair to say that no one executes a sponge bath
quite the way that I do.

I've earned my black belt and a PhD
in the ancient art of sponge-bathery.
Tomorrow's job?
Bucket laundry.

Is my plumbing broken?
Is my bathroom being renovated?

No.
This is about me using my voice,
this is about those who have no choice,
and the reason I do this is to make you think;
How much water was used when you were last at the
    kitchen sink?
Between your ingrained habits, the taxes you pay,
and ability of your grandchildren to freely play
in a lake devoid of blue-green algae,
between the energy used to pump sacred life to your
    home through subterranean water highways,
between all of these things,
can you make a link?

Twenty-five litres a day is all I'm allowed,
this manic month of scribbling and jotting.
I am the calorie counter of the water world
and now I realise, with the sharp clarity and the sudden
    compulsion
of someone who's rapidly losing her footing
on the crumbling sandstone at the brink of an OCD
    chasm,
why diets never work.

I want to etch on your minds with a water-based ink,
I want you all to be thinking about how much water
    you use
and how much you abuse.
I've been labelled alarmist, a dirty hippie, and more
By those trolling from the far side of a distant keyboard.

Now as I measure out bathing water,
I can almost already feel the sleek ribbons of cascading
      warmth
soon to be delivered by my trusty yoghurt container.
This sponge bath is earned, and I'll enjoy it more
than ever before that I've reached out to turn on that
      shower dial.

Up the stairs with my bucket, careful not to slop,
I can't afford to waste a single drop.
Into the bathroom, ready to go
with my luxury steaming H2 ... Oh!!
No ...

Tragedy has struck.
In my haste, I have stumbled and spilled my bucket.
I watch my efforts drain away,
blue gold on porcelain in the bottom of the tub.
Now I must walk downstairs, measure out more water,
and return to the stove with it.
The novelty has worn off and by this stage,
I'm over it.

Still.
I walk down 16 stairs,
and it sure as hell beats 16 miles.

From a sun-baked village on a dusty road,
a woman with a jug on her head, she goes.
Where this woman she goes,
she walks with her hopes,
she wonders if anyone hears her story.

In three short days, my stand of solidarity comes to end

but I will not forget.

Her story echoes in every drip of a leaky shower head,
in every careless flush.
The weight of her clay jug sits on my shoulders
each time I see somebody turn their back
on a running tap.

Tomorrow's wars won't be fought over a thirst for oil,
but over thirst,
in and of itself.

With three days to go, I'm struck by the irony
that water makes up
70 percent of my body.

So when the wells run dry and our fields turn to dust,
I wonder,
will they be coming to tap me?

———

To view the video of this poem, follow the link below or scan the QR code at the beginning of the poem.

alinasiegfried.com/water-poem

THE PERSONAL IS THE
POWERFUL

5

—————————————

A FOUR-YEAR-OLD'S GUIDE TO FRAMING

AFTER SIX WEEKS OF A SORT OF STRANGE, SURREAL GROUNDHOG Day during New Zealand's countrywide COVID-19 lockdown, in May 2020 we narrowly avoided a monumental meltdown in our household. Having been stuck in the repetitive pattern of waking up each day and trying to come up with new home-based activities to do with the kids, while also trying to squeeze in work and book writing, the boundaries of time had become hazy. Just as during the summer holidays, with long, lazy hours spent in enjoyment, when you might find yourself asking what day it is, my days had all been blurring into one. As a consequence, I had spent a good portion of a Friday in May thinking that it was Saturday already. Our son's fourth birthday was on the Sunday. Being a day ahead of myself, I spent all afternoon excitedly telling him that the following day was his birthday. I even put him to bed around 7:30 p.m. with hearty encouragement to enjoy his last sleep as a three-year-old, and that in the morning, he would be four. He went to sleep with a big smile on his face. And then my partner came home from a gruelling trip to the grocery store and duly informed me that it was indeed only Friday.

Many facepalms ensued. How could I have gotten a day ahead? And more importantly, how was I going to fix this and avoid heartbreak and outrage the next day? After a fair amount of debate about how much weight to put on the situation—my instinct being to play it down and signal that it was a silly mistake in the hopes that our son would follow my lead, while my partner thought that I should front foot it and make a big deal of apologising profusely to our boy—we agreed upon a plan somewhere in the middle. I would tell our son of my mistake, explain that I was really sorry, let it sink in for a moment, and then drop the big exciting twist: today would be a practice-run birthday! Complete with blueberry pancakes for breakfast, with a candle on top.

Without realising it, we had employed the use of *framing* to placate a distraught young child. And for the most part, it worked. Many parents would have done just as I did in this situation, without a second thought. We want to avoid unnecessary drama, and silver linings make for happier memories, so we frame things in a positive light where possible. While we might instinctively know the power of framing with our children, adults tend to forget how important it is in driving our attitudes and behaviours. Unless we've built a career in politics, journalism, or social psychology, many of us don't readily question the framing behind the messages that are presented to us every day. Yet most strategic framing is no more refined or sophisticated than the simple redirection of attention that I used with my son. Frames are littered throughout our language, telling micro-stories with just a few words. Their great power is in their simplicity and in this sense, words can change the world. In order to shift broad narratives, we need to start with the very basics.

The way in which we frame a problem plays a big role in how we think about potential solutions. During my time working on freshwater advocacy in Saskatchewan, I came across the Water Soft Path, a framework of freshwater management originally applied to energy in the 1970s by Amory Lovins.[1] The framework is largely based on reframing the role of freshwater in our lives, describing water as a service rather than a product. Let me ask you the question: do we really need to flush our toilets and irrigate our crops with fresh water? Or is it rather that the need we are looking to fulfil is the removal of human waste and growing of abundant food? In the first of these scenarios, water is a *resource* in and of itself; in the second it is framed as a *service agent*. By that simple reframe, we can investigate problems from new angles. Composting toilets and grey water recycling systems might provide the service of waste removal as an alternative to the use of drinking-quality water. Indoor growing systems and the adoption of regenerative agricultural methods that hold more moisture in the soil might be alternatives to widespread irrigation use. The framework also elevates natural ecosystems as legitimate or even priority users of water. This is a big jump in perspective from the predominant social and economic narratives that suggest nature is freely available for humans to use, and it challenges the notion of human centrality on the planet. The reframe puts the needs of natural ecosystems—which we depend upon for life on this planet to continue—on an equal pedestal with the functioning of industry, agriculture, and other aspects of our economy. It challenges us to think about what it is that we value. It is after all that which we value that we seek to protect and uphold.

————

It was in central Canada that I cut my teeth on framing, but it was in my next role that I got the chance to really hone my skills. After living abroad for four years, I felt the pull to return back to home soil. I packed up my life in Canada and moved back to New Zealand, gravitating towards the capital city of Wellington. Then in January 2011, I walked into New Zealand's Parliament buildings as an eager and earnest young woman ready to change the world. I had accepted a job with Parliamentary Services that was focused on developing and supporting environmental issues campaigns led by members of Parliament in one of New Zealand's more progressive political parties. The role presented the fascinating challenge of working closely with politicians in what was ultimately a non-partisan, taxpayer-funded role. While it was tough at times to remain impartial in my work and focus purely on the issues at hand, I came to realise afterwards the unique viewpoint it had afforded me. I learned to start thinking about solving environmental challenges from a neutral standpoint—a muscle that I sorely needed to practise flexing. The experience allowed me to transform from a staunch young activist into someone a little more nuanced in my views.

Nowhere has the power of framing been more effective than within the political realm. Politicians have forever been choosy with their words, knowing the power of spinning a story in a particular way to elicit a desired response from the public. The party I worked alongside shared a great deal of my values, and for the most part, they grounded their policies and decisions in their values. Confident that I was contributing towards positive social and environmental change, I threw myself into learning all I could about political framing, and in particular values-based framing, which I talk about more in the next chapter. I read George Lakoff's 2004 book *Don't Think of an Elephant!*, which is considered somewhat of a bible for progressively focused political nerds.[2] New Zealand has a mixed-member proportional system of central governance, which means that members from many different political parties are represented in Parliament. Being in Opposition, a lot of my work was focused on campaigns that promoted alternative policies to those of the government that was in power. Given my experience in Canada and roots in resource management, I worked primarily on freshwater and other environmental campaigns. New Zealand has seen a drastic decline of freshwater quality in the past few decades, thanks mainly to the cumulative effects of intensified agriculture and widespread synthetic fertiliser use in many regions, and this was a big focus of the party's election campaigns. Wherever possible, we made efforts to frame things in terms of duty of care, unity, and protecting what we love, in recognition that when you are trying to sway people's views (or votes), it is more effective to frame things in terms of what you are for, than what you are against.

This positive approach to framing was remarkably effective in contributing to New Zealand eliminating COVID-19 from the country after the first outbreak in mid-2020. In the early days of the coronavirus pandemic, many countries adopted frames of war in their public messaging. We heard obvious statements such as "we are at war" and "the battle against coronavirus," along with more subtle references to patients being "struck down," medical professionals being "frontline" workers, or different countries "gaining ground." British Prime Minister Boris Johnson spoke of a "fight" in which each and every citizen was "directly enlisted." These sorts of frames subtly suggested that COVID-19 was an enemy that we need to throw our arsenal at and overcome through combative means, rather than working together with communities and other countries to stem the spread of the virus and find constructive public health solutions. It bestowed evil intent upon the virus as if it were attacking human populations out of some conscious, malicious motive to destroy us all, rather than simply behaving exactly as a virus does. It is telling to look back over a year later, and observe that it is the countries whose leaders were most aggressive in their use of strongman war rhetoric that have been least successful at stemming the spread of the virus.

Rather than adopting battle framing, New Zealand's Prime Minister Jacinda Ardern set the tone from the get-go with frames of solidarity and collective responsibility. In the early weeks in New Zealand, we heard constantly that we were all in the same boat. Ardern's brilliant use of the phrase "team of five million" to refer to New Zealand's entire population is one that will go down in the history books as a grand, unifying frame that helped New Zealand eliminate the first wave of the virus. The nation's isolated location without land borders certainly helped to keep it out, but within the country, the population's widespread compliance with directives to stay at home was underpinned by a sense of unity. Note that it wasn't an *army* of five million who were focused on conflict, it was a *team*—a group of individuals that came together to work towards a common goal. Ardern's choice of words showed strategic use of a frame to appeal to values of unity, collectivism, and cooperation. Likewise, her framing of medical professionals, nurses, grocery store employees, and public transport workers as "essential workers" rather than "frontline workers" suggested a crucial dependency upon these people by wider society, evoking feelings of affinity and interdependence, rather than likening them to soldiers.

The power of framing to unite is matched by its power to divide, though not always by the most direct or obvious means. Think of the phrase "Make America Great Again," the infamous slogan of the 2016 election that saw a ruthless businessman and reality TV star gain the highest seat in American politics. The phrase suggests that things are not all well in the land of the free, and plays on a sense of nostalgia and the national narrative of American excellence. It's a brilliant frame. Taken at face value, it's a great idea. What American wouldn't want their country to be great? However, whatever your political leanings, I think it's fair to say Trump's presidency was marked by a level of division that has not been seen in the United States for some decades. At the core of the narrative behind "Make America Great Again" was a finger pointed squarely at those who were supposedly to blame for America not being great any more: immigrants, people of colour, Democrats, big city liberals, LGBTQ+ folk, or whatever real or imagined "other" was perceived to be a threat to many people's perceptions of the American way of life. What Donald Trump did was tell a highly compelling story that resonated with a sector of the population who had become deeply distrustful of establishment politicians who they saw as out of touch with their lives. In this regard, his slogan actually did a great job of unifying a lot of people. But the frame itself came to be a proxy for his divisive brand of politics that sought to pitch that unified group against virtually anyone who dared challenge him. Never mind that Trump's life and career is wildly out of touch with many of the Americans who voted for him. What mattered most was that he was telling a story that resonated, and that he wrapped it all up in a genius frame. He also grounded many of his messages and policies to appeal to the values of his voter base—values of hard work, conformity, national security, and respect for tradition.

The two examples above show the power of simple frames within the political realm, wielding starkly different results. As the old adage goes, with great power comes great responsibility and it's as true as ever when we are choosing how we frame any given message. Of course, we don't all work in politics. Many of us don't even work in jobs where framing is something that we need to actively think about. Some of us don't work at all, at least not under the standard definition of *work* as trading time, services, or products for money. But whatever we do with our lives and time on this Earth, we are constantly framing all our communications while simultaneously being susceptible to how others choose to frame theirs. It is in our choice of words, the language that we use to describe people, and in the ways we talk about our work and societies. We can achieve a lot towards seeing a more just and equitable world by simply paying more attention to how the messages we hear are framed, and questioning the motives behind those who craft them. We can also achieve a lot by choosing our words wisely in everyday conversation, by framing our visions of change in terms of what we believe in rather than what we are against, and by grounding ourselves in our values. We build and change the world and people's perceptions of it through active framing and reframing.

6

THE VALUE OF VALUES

IMAGINE THAT YOU'RE HEADING TO THE CHECKOUT OF A LARGE department store such as Walmart or Target with a few items of discounted clothing. When you get to the cashier, instead of asking if you would like to make a small donation to a charity along with your purchase today, he nonchalantly asks you if you would like an additional two dollars discounted off your purchase in exchange for polluting a village's water supply in Bangladesh. Would you say yes to that offer? Would you consider that two dollars off your clothing purchase was worth poisoning someone else's drinking water? I'm guessing the majority of people would be taken aback, and decline the clerk's polite offer of an additional discount. We would say no because to say yes would be a direct and conscious affront to our values and sense of morality. The fact remains that it is highly likely that when we purchase ultra-cheap clothing, we are somewhere along the line supporting the externalisation of costs to poorer countries that is built into the global fast fashion industry. The difference is in the framing. The quid pro quo of the price tag may include the pollution of rivers and lakes, the release of harmful chemicals into the atmosphere, child labour, slave labour, and human trafficking. It also contributes to unsafe working conditions such as those that contributed to the collapse of the eight-storey Rana Plaza complex in Bangladesh in 2013, which killed 1134 garment workers. Presented with the frame that our cost-cutting purchase harms other people, we might pause to think. But these parts of the story are hidden, and instead the frame that is used is "60% off!" or "three for $10!".

I have on my living room wall a framed copy of an infographic by David McCandless and Stefanie Posavec that displays the two sides of the traditional political spectrum as a balanced set of scales.[1] On each side, the values and virtues that both the left and the right hold dear are contrasted with opposing ones that are equally valid and dearly held by those on the other side, across a number of different societal issues. Where the left tends to place value on strong ethics, the right leans towards moral absolutes. Where the left might consider that healthy, thriving communities are grounded in equality, cooperation, and empathy, the right sees freedom, self-reliance, and opportunity as the foundations of a healthy society. Where progressives might teach self-nurturance and a sense of curiosity to their children, traditional conservatives may instil a sense of discipline and strength of character. Each of these values and virtues holds merit. Self-nurturance is a useful skill, as is self-discipline. Equality is a cornerstone of a thriving society, as is the freedom to be in control of your own life. Ethics and morals are both important.

I have this infographic on my wall to remind me daily that while I may not agree with people who think differently to myself, I can at least understand on some level how they got there. It frames things in terms of what it is that they care about, rather than relying on the rhetoric of my social media feed about what they stand against. I can see that the views that I might be tempted to label as hateful, ignorant, or greedy are rooted in a set of guiding values and moral principles that are simply different from my own. It might be hard for me to understand and to resonate with, but at least on some level I know in a general sense why other people are the way they are and why they behave as they do. Of course, we don't live in a vacuum, and the usefulness of a left vs right political spectrum is increasingly becoming questioned as we look around at the state of many of our democracies. Discounting those with extreme or fundamentalist views either way, most people generally fall somewhere in the middle of the spectrum with more progressive or conservative views on different issues, although this varies depending upon country and population. It is the majority of the population in the middle of the bell curve who hold the real power in shifting narratives to address systemic issues.

On any given issue, our positions are heavily influenced by our values, which act as a set of guiding principles directing our thoughts and behaviours, and reassuring us that our way of thinking is right, just, and good. We each hold hundreds of values that we place varying degrees of importance upon, often with their roots in the morals that we learned in childhood. Our values form a core part of our identities. They guide our decision-making. They help us find and rally around communities of interest. Sometimes our values may be in opposition to each other, and we need to make a decision about which value we will prioritise in any given situation. For example, in many ways I consider myself a pretty loyal person. But I also love experiencing the most out of life and seeking adventures that bring me joy. So if I am faced with a hypothetical situation of going to listen to a friend's boring public talk on some obscure topic in which I have no interest or accepting an invitation to go on a spontaneous night-time mission to view some glow-worms with a new acquaintance, I need to make a decision about whether I will prioritise my value of loyalty or those of adventure and joyful experience. We tend to hold some values more strongly than others, and prioritise them more frequently.

Loosely speaking, our values may fall into two categories, and it is through activating those in the first category that we have the best chance to enact systemic change. Intrinsic values are those core values that most people hold close to their heart—values of love, kindness, affinity, connection, and community. Extrinsic values are those that are more externally focused—those of power, conformity, image, popularity, and the modern-day, conventional understanding of success. In his ground-breaking book *Lost Connections*, which investigates the root causes of the mental health epidemic afflicting many Western cultures, author Johann Hari refers to the latter category as "junk values." In the same way that eating an excess of nutrient-poor, processed, and sugar-laden junk foods can be detrimental to our physical health, consuming an excess of extrinsic, junk values is detrimental to mental health. It feels good at the time —we get a hit from power and popularity the same way we get a sugar rush. But as we know with junk food, it's not good for us in the long term. We receive messages that activate our extrinsic values day and night from the moment we are old enough to understand language. It is important to win at all costs. Becoming an influencer on Instagram is the key to fame and fortune. Working long hours to beat that competitor to market is worth the sacrifice of time spent with family. From advertising and the media, to our education system and the halls of political power, we are bombarded with messages that reinforce a harmful narrative of what constitutes happiness and success. Rooted in the notion of scarcity and competition, the promotion of these extrinsic values underpins our economic system of modern-day capitalism. Ironically, a study in 2016 found that when asked about their values, the majority of people said they care more about intrinsic, compassionate values like helpfulness and equality while at the same time they mistakenly assumed that other people care more about selfish, extrinsic values such as wealth, public image, and success.[2] So generally speaking, our perception is that we ourselves are good, kind people, but that others are more selfishly oriented.

Our values play a significant role in how we respond to messages that are framed a certain way. Consider the terms *illegal aliens* vs *undocumented refugees*, *environmental regulation* vs *environmental protection*, *free market economics* vs *unfettered capitalism*, or *welfare state* vs *social safety net*. While each of these pairs of words generally refers to the same thing, each frame has very different connotations as it draws on different values. Someone who holds and prioritises the values of empathy and compassion is unlikely to appreciate the frame of *illegal aliens* in reference to people who have fled oppressive regimes. Someone who holds and prioritises the values of discipline, self-reliance, and perseverance may not respond positively to the suggestion of a *social safety net*, believing that those on welfare simply do not try hard enough. The words that we choose to describe problems and solutions influence whether or not people agree that there is a problem in the first place, and whether or not they are supportive of the solution. Since George Lakoff's *Don't Think of an Elephant!* and a number of subsequent efforts to highlight the power of values-based framing, those seeking progressive change have been increasingly framing their communications to activate the values of the populations they are looking to influence. But on many fronts, the progress is slow. Overwhelmingly global conversations around the need to address climate change are still focused on the science, policy, and technical details, when the reality is that for most of us, facts and figures are not a strong motivator for action. The science is of course a crucial piece of the puzzle; it provides the objectivity that serves as an agreed reference point. But without a widespread culture shift, the science alone will not be enough to drive us to curb emissions. The past forty years of underwhelming global response have shown that. We will not collectively act on a reasoned case to protect the environment, but rather because we are moved to do so by story-driven messaging that speaks to our values. The same is true of social challenges—statistics around poverty, inequality, and systemic racism do not provide enough impetus for change. We need to appeal to the heart, rather than the head.

What do you think of when I say the phrase "family values"? In much of our popular culture, driven by political framing and echoed in the media, this phrase has come to be associated with values of hierarchy, authority, discipline, and tradition. Yet when I look at my own family, the values that I hold dear are those of love, fulfilment, playfulness, protection, community, responsibility, and that much-debated word, *freedom*. The word *morality* is similarly loaded with connotations of strictness, conformity, and religious observation. But what about progressive morals? Recently I saw a picture of a Black Lives Matter protestor holding a sign that read "If you aren't outraged, you aren't paying attention." The point being made is that the disproportionate taking of black lives by police officers isn't so much a question of race relations, law and order, or misunderstanding; it is an issue of moral injustice. Outrage is an appropriate and necessary moral reaction to the sort of systemic racism that cavalierly takes lives and enables a large proportion of the population and media to not bat an eyelid at yet another loss of a black life.

If we are to overcome the collective inertia we feel in how to address our most complex problems, we need to start framing climate change, inequality, food insecurity, the destruction of natural ecosystems, the loss of indigenous sovereignty, and the trampling of human rights around the world not as scientific or political issues to address, but as the *moral challenges* of our time. The key to gaining widespread buy-in to address systemic challenges lies not in guilting people into action or appealing to rationality but in framing our intrinsic values and activating a deep sense of collective responsibility. We have a moral obligation to protect the planet we call home. We have a moral obligation to prevent further extinctions of plant and animal species. We have a moral obligation to ensure that every person on Earth is given an equal chance to achieve a happy and healthy life, regardless of race, class, social status, religion, place of birth, or other limiting factors. We have a moral obligation to support the most vulnerable members of our communities and neighbourhoods in which we live. In each of these cases, we need to encourage action not because it is based on logic and reason, but because it is simply the right thing to do. We need to be telling the stories about why we care so much in the first place, appealing to people's values with a sense of passion and hope. While anger and protest certainly have their place, systemic change requires us to speak loudly to what we value, rather than only respond to what we don't. Think about the daily language you choose, and how it either reinforces or negates the kind of world you want to live in. Living out our intrinsic values is contagious, as others implicitly receive permission to live out their own. The more we experience grace, mercy, compassion, and kindness at the hands of others, especially those who disagree with our views, the more likely we are to reflect those values back out into the world.

When I started working in politics, I had a lot of faith in our political system and in our politicians. After a while, however, I felt a creeping sense of disillusionment with the system of government that was running our country. Grace, mercy, and kindness tend to be lacking in the internal workings of most political systems. While often the communications I was crafting and perpetuating were grounded in intrinsic values, these messages were just as often accompanied by some sort of finger pointing, laying of blame, and convenient omission of the complexities of the issues at play. Picking easy targets, scoring media wins, and over-simplifying complex problems were tactics that were all too common from politicians from all sides of the spectrum. On one hand, I was speaking of how much New Zealanders love our natural environment and lamenting that our children could no longer swim in the same rivers that we did as kids. On the other, I was vilifying farmers with frames of "dirty dairying" and lambasting the government for "selling Kiwis down the river." Too often, I found myself disproportionately criticising and pointing out all that was flawed in the government's policy. I began to tire of the regular petty squabbling that I saw in the debating chamber, and became uncomfortable with the level of "othering" that I saw towards those who didn't agree. It struck me that once they gained power to govern, the Opposition politicians I was working with would inherit the responsibility to solve the same set of overwhelmingly complex, messy, and interconnected problems and issues that they were so criticising the government for failing to fix in a quick and simple manner. It felt highly hypocritical. While I held no animosity towards the individual politicians—after all, they are overwhelmingly good people who are just cogs trying to operate in a broken machine

—I came to realise how much harm the dynamic duo of politics and media can achieve to sow the seeds of division, disillusionment, and outrage directed at whoever was the easy target of the day. Sometimes of course there are clear culprits in exacerbating a problem, for example when a corporation actively lobbies governments against environmental protections, or someone acts in a corrupt manner to subvert the democratic process. But more often, the problems that politicians are seeking to solve are highly systemic in nature, and there are no easy wins and no clear offenders. My time in Parliament taught me to take whatever political reporting I hear with a grain of salt, and to question the spin and framing that goes into every message, even from those we broadly agree with.

The adversarial state of our politics is somewhat understandable and is in itself a systemic problem. When all you have space for is a two-sentence media sound bite, there is little scope to go into the complexities and interconnections of any given problem that you're trying to solve, so you'd best get across some version of it while you can. Politicians know that they are predominantly aiming to reach the audiences that are more likely to favour them, and it's mighty tempting to ruthlessly point the finger at others to win over voters. But this mentality and the abhorrent behaviour that it sometimes promotes is leading to serious consequences. Our democracies are becoming more broken every year. Faith in our political institutions is waning and voter turnout has declined sharply in many countries over the past forty years.[3] After three years in Parliament, I realised that for me to tell the kind of integrated and nuanced stories that I wanted to tell, I was in the entirely wrong arena. Politics is not the place to change deeply ingrained systems. It is the place to change individual policies and laws, but for systemic change to occur the bigger shift needs to be in the cultural mindset of the voting public. Politicians after all respond to the will and demands of the electorate. So we need to collectively get used to thinking about how we can make room for more voices, act and communicate in accordance with our values, move beyond black-and-white thinking, and adopt a truly collaborative mindset towards solving problems.

7

EATING YOUR OWN DOG FOOD

THE DAY I PUSHED SEND ON THE FIRST DRAFT OF MY TEDxChristchurch talk to the event speaker coach, I knew that I wasn't 100 percent comfortable with it and that something was missing. Telling the story of how I had discovered the world of slam poetry and its power to shift thinking and drive behaviour change, I had at one point casually alluded to something crazy going on in my life at that time, and rushed on to say that I had learned a great deal about myself. It was completely vague, giving no clues as to what had been happening, why it was crazy, or what I had learned. The speaker coach emailed back within hours, and straight up called me out for omitting the details. I had known on some level that it was poor, incomplete storytelling and that it would leave an audience wanting to know more, but I had been desperately trying to avoid doing something that was scary as hell for me: coming out as gay to a live audience of seven hundred people.

The crazy thing I referred to in that first draft of my talk was my coming to a personal realisation in my late twenties that I had been in deep denial about my sexuality for well over a decade, and that it was no longer a viable option to keep my true self hidden. I had consequently ended a relationship with a kind man who I cared about deeply and with whom I had bought a house just months earlier. I had been going through the painstaking process of separating my life with that of a baffled and heartbroken partner who had been completely blindsided. In the following months, I was simultaneously processing feelings of elation and freedom, immense guilt, and confusion as to how I could have buried such a crucial part of myself in the furthermost recesses of my psyche. My life was a shambles as my story of self that I had so carefully crafted for so long was crumbling spectacularly all around me. I was raised in a Christian home and remember struggling as a teenager with the tensions between the teachings of the church and the inconvenient attractions I was feeling towards classmates at my all-girls high school. The conflicting stories of my identity had been completely at odds with each other. And then suddenly at almost twenty-eight, feelings of long-suppressed shame were once again coming to the surface. But this time the shame was not directed at the fact that I was gay, but rather at having lied to myself for so long about it.

I recall confiding in a close friend a few weeks before I told my partner. After having uttered those two tiny little words for the first time—"I'm gay"—I told her there were two simultaneous, opposing thoughts going through my head. The first was *Oh my god, there's no turning back*; the second, *Thank god, there's no turning back*. Both of those things rang true for me. Torn between trying to respect my partner's feelings and wanting to get out there and start exploring my new identity, it was a tumultuous year filled with a great deal of personal reflection and learning. Poetry was my outlet, and I processed a lot of the feelings that were bubbling up by spouting them from the stage every Sunday evening. It was like a form of therapy, with dozens of audience therapists actively listening. I made many mistakes along the way. My partner was deeply hurt at the speed with which I had seemingly moved on, being unaware of the months of internal processing that I had already gone through before choosing that fateful Friday afternoon to make my big announcement. Looking back, I realised I had often put my own needs and feelings before his, and felt a certain degree of regret at how I had acted.

By omitting this particular story from my TEDx talk, I was trying to avoid being vulnerable and coming out to a large room full of people, and indeed any number of others who might stumble upon the talk online in the future. It was 2013, before we had marriage equality in New Zealand, and there was still a significant degree of prejudice towards LGBTQ+ people from large sectors of society who have since mellowed somewhat. But by hiding the details I was burying a hugely powerful part of my story—a story that contained lessons of universal relevance, from the importance of treating people well in difficult circumstances to being gentle with yourself as you let your own stories unfold. The great irony of this situation is that my talk emphasised the power of authenticity in storytelling, and there I was trying to avoid being authentic. In the software development community, the phrase "eating your own dog food" is commonplace as a metaphor for using the software that you build within your own company and teams. Internet rumour has it that the phrase originated in the 1970s when Canadian actor Lorne Greene claimed he fed Alpo dog food to his own dogs. Another version of the story tells of the president of a different pet food company who was said to eat a can of the company's dog food at shareholders' meetings. Whatever the origins, within software development, eating your own dog food is a way of discovering first-hand the bugs, the kinks, or the less-than-optimal user experience. After all, if you're not willing to use your own software, then why should anyone else buy it? For me, the process of getting up on stage in front of seven hundred people to speak about authenticity and telling my own authentic story felt a lot like eating my own dog food.

———

Nothing inspires us more than narratives of personal experience. The power of a person relaying the triumphs and traumas that they have faced in all their messy human glory far outweighs that of general examples. When we give voice to our stories, people can see the humanity and commonalities between us. And it is not only the receiver of the story that benefits—by carefully dissecting our experiences and holding the pieces up to the light, we can learn a great deal about ourselves. Through careful and compassionate investigation, we have the opportunity to reframe the stories of our past, recasting ourselves or others in a different role. We might realise that in that heroic tale that we've been carrying all those years, we may at times have acted a little villainous. Or that the person who had hurt us, and who we had consequently cast into the role of villain, was in fact going through a great deal of personal turbulence themselves and had been doing the best they could to get through it without any harm intended.

Despite the terror of coming out so publicly, telling the story of discovering a part of myself that had been a source of shame for so long was a profoundly cathartic experience. It was a step that helped pave the way to healing the wounds of my past, and accepting who I was. A by-product of becoming more self-aware of our stories and the way that they influence our lives is that we become more authentic, which in turn makes us better storytellers. It's a self-perpetuating cycle. For better or worse, the personal is the powerful and undeniably influences the collective, as it paves the way for other hidden stories to come to the surface. I'll never know how many others might have been inspired to share their own stories after hearing me share my own.

The evening after my TEDx talk had been successfully delivered, embracing the full messiness of my journey and the power of spoken word, my leap from the world of political storytelling began. During a late-night conversation with a friend at the afterparty, I learned that a Wellington-based software start-up was looking for a communications person to support them with a global crowdfunding campaign. An insistent follow-up email to my friend the next day landed both of my feet on the ground in this new world. Within weeks, I went from my stable public sector role to embracing the title of "Communications Wrangler" with a small, nimble social enterprise, cutting my salary in half, and with zero idea what I was going to do after my six-month contract was up. Loomio developed software to help groups to facilitate discussion and make decisions together online. Any member of a group could propose an idea or course of action, which others could then comment and vote on, bringing transparency, efficiency, and genuine, democratic participation to decision-making. It was a simple, beautiful idea with its roots in the Occupy movement, which had not long before seen millions around the world rallying against social and economic inequality. In many ways Loomio was the polar opposite of the slow-moving Parliamentary behemoth I had left behind. In a time when many people have become disillusioned with our systems of democracy, the themes we were rallying around were those of equality of voice, efficiency, radical authenticity, and equality of access to the decision-making table. Inspired by the hand signals used in Occupy camps around the world to collectively make decisions in an emergent movement, the purpose of Loomio was to capture the same collaborative culture online and scale it massively with open source software. While the goal wasn't necessarily consensus, the platform provided a means for every stakeholder to share their thoughts and be heard. There were no goodies or baddies here, just authentic participation. We ate our own dog food daily by using the software to make internal team decisions. The platform itself had been translated into over thirty languages, mainly by enthusiastic volunteers in the open source software community, and we had all manner of groups using it from local food co-ops and start-up teams, to citizen democracy groups organising to fight austerity measures in Greece, and the London School of Economics experimenting with the idea of crowdsourcing a written constitution for the UK. Our own local council used Loomio to consult the public on a proposed new alcohol management strategy for the central city, gathering diverse views and enabling the public to vote on proposed courses of action. As a core venture of the Enspiral network, Loomio was also used by this agile and emergent community to organise, discuss projects, and make decisions together. Personally, I started to see my own narratives shifting around how groups, organisations, perhaps even whole countries could determine their futures together in a meaningful way. A new story was developing for me over who held the power, and how they could wield it.

Operating as a non-hierarchical cooperative, Loomio had a culture of bringing your whole self and any story you wanted to share into the workplace. It was a refreshing alternative to the story of the "heropreneur," which so often dominates the narrative of tech start-ups. There was no one founder elevated on a pedestal, whose story was to be the face of the organisation. Everything that the company stood for flew in the face of that kind of hero worship culture. Loomio was about allowing every person's views to come to the table, whether it be a boardroom table, a volunteer organiser's kitchen table, or a metaphorical one around which people in many different locations could converge. We began each team meeting with a check-in on how we were each feeling that day. It was less to do with what we were working on, but more of a chance to share things that might be going on at home, celebrate any wins from the previous week, or let the team know what was on our minds in general. With the software still in its infancy, I was charged with leading the communications strategy surrounding a US$100,000 non-equity crowdfunding campaign to take it global. Central to our strategy was telling the human stories of both the users and the members of our team, so one of my first courses of action was to sit down with each of the twelve or so core team members and ask a bunch of questions about their life story. To tell the story of Loomio, an organisation focused on authentic participation by all members of any group, community, or team, I needed to know the stories of the humans driving it. I wanted to understand their journeys and how they came to be working to help reconfigure the mechanisms of participatory decision-making. Each person's hopes, dreams, passions, and experiences played a role in defining the story of the organisation as a collective, which in turn played a role in redefining the narratives surrounding democracy at a global scale. Some of the team came from traditional business backgrounds, others from the arts, and one or two were radical anarchists. Everyone learned a great deal from hearing each other's stories.

When my six-month Loomio contract came to an end in May 2014, I started chatting with a few people I had met through the Enspiral network, who were in the early stages of launching a new venture. Two American brothers, Matthew and Brian Monahan, along with their friend and co-founder Yoseph Ayele, were looking to create some sort of pathway to New Zealand for high-impact entrepreneurial leaders who were experimenting at the leading edges of technology, environmental protection, social justice, climate change response, and systems thinking. I came on board as their first hire, to help craft the narrative of New Zealand as a petri dish for innovative experiments in impact. Over the next few years, in collaboration with Immigration New Zealand, we would develop the Edmund Hillary Fellowship (EHF), a global community of fellows comprising entrepreneurs, investors, innovators, artists, activists, storytellers, farmers, filmmakers, and other professionals who were driven to make systemic change in the world. In one of the several interviews that I had for the role, the founders expressed that it was my spoken word poetry that had captured their attention, and that they wanted me to bring that level of creative communication to the company. Never had I imagined when I had stood on that dimly lit stage in the Canadian prairies four years earlier to perform some poetry about water conservation and behaviour change, that the act of sharing my heartfelt, vulnerable stories with a motley crowd of literary nerds would lead me here. I relished in the moment when I called my mother and announced how that little poetry hobby I had been dabbling in had landed me "a real job."

POETIC INTERLUDE 2

BIG WORLD, SMALL PLANET: THE REMIX

Watch a video of this poem

75,000 years ago,
on a high plateau in what will one day become Ethiopia,
a woman scans the barren ground for seeds and berries.
Tightens the furs binding baby to her breast,
oblivious that she holds in her hands
the future of the human race.

On the brink of extinction,

humanity's population has dwindled to a mere
     handful—
perhaps just a few thousand of us remain on the face of
     the Earth.

Just a blip in human history, merely a moment in time,
it is the story we never hear about how we almost
     disappeared.

Some 10,000 years ago
upon the alluvial plains of Mesopotamia,
an ageing farmer gazes out across a golden field of
     barley.
The ancient ones speak of a time when food was
     foraged from the wild,
but he has planted with intent.
Master of his own destiny, he is blissfully unaware
that this very moment in time marks the inception of
     humanity's ascent.

The following millennia will see us at our best and
     worst,
from conquests and crusades, witch trials and slaves,
to renaissance arts, mathematics, medicine, and the
     discoveries of space.

In 1804, on the filthy wooden floor of a London slum,
a young mother unwittingly gives birth to the billionth
     living member of the human race.

Forty years later
her son mops his sodden brow,
shovelling coal into the insatiable fiery mouth
of a shining new steam engine.

Soot black-eyed and bone-broke weary,
he is building the future of industry,
he is progressing the human race.

A 1950s housewife rides shotgun in a '57 Chevrolet
     Bel Air.
Sits proudly beside her husband,
who is among the one sixth of American working age
     adults to be
employed by the automobile industry at the time.
Oblivious to unintended consequences,
they are paving freeways across the future.

In 2008, from the elevated porch of a longhouse in
     Borneo,
an elder surveys the thick dark smoke
blanketing a land where forest fires are foreign.
The rainforest slash and burn makes way for
     monocultural palm oil.
The fires burn so vast that the collective smoke would
     account
for 30 percent of global greenhouse gas emissions that
     year.

It is this day,
and we are no longer unaware;
no longer averting our eyes from the caged canary
that has been lying unmoving for quite some time now.

It is this day,
and the Earth is submitting her invoices
for the streets we have paved with gold,
for every incremental blip in human progress,
and payment needs to be underwritten by a

monumental mindshift.

It is time for us to step up and respect the boundaries
of just how far we can push this planet;
become stewards of our collective futures
and recognise just how much our livelihoods depend
     on it.

We live in a globalised community,
a big world on a small planet,
where our every flutter of a butterfly wing
can either serve to strengthen the hurricane
or fuel the winds of change.
And like it or not, these days
we make our homes in each other's backyards.

The Nigerian farmer whose dreams wash away with the
     soils
after every season's floods, the rain no longer soaking
     the earth,
that man is your neighbour.
The machete-wielding clear-cutter lives in the Amazon
     basin next door.
Look into the eyes of the Congolese youth,
risking life and limb in civil conflict to mine the
     minerals for our mobile phones,
and you will find a brother.

This is not about sacrifice,
but about unleashing our full potential.
Not about saying no, but about embracing a resounding
     Yes.
This is about building the house of humanity with hard
     hats and steel-toed boots;

travelling the mountain roads of our destiny with guard
    rails to mark out the cliffs.

This is about humanity moving out of mama's home
and learning to do our own laundry,
emerging from adolescence into adulthood,
embracing responsibility.

A hundred billion moments of human progress have
    brought us to this point.
One hundred billion blips.

In late 2017 in Wellington, New Zealand,
A woman enters a fertility clinic with bated breath.

Nine months later,
scanning the future for some berries of hope and seeds
    of change,
tightening the sling binding baby to my breast,
I hold one tiny contribution to the future of the human
    race.

In every blink of my daughter's eyes,
a blip in history.
In every blip, a reminder
of a global citizen in the making,
already, taking notes.

———

To view the video of this poem, follow the link below or scan the QR
code at the beginning of the poem.

alinasiegfried.com/bwsp-the-remix

8

A COLLECTIVE HERO'S JOURNEY

WHEN I FIRST PERFORMED THE POEM "BIG WORLD, SMALL Planet: The Remix," I was five months pregnant and the daughter I refer to at the end had yet to draw breath. The original ending, which I've since necessarily had to change for the poem to remain relevant, referred not to a born child but to the tiny contribution towards the future of the human race that I still held within my belly. The performance was at an impact summit hosted by our team at the Edmund Hillary Fellowship (EHF), which brought together systems thinkers, government officials, and globally minded folks from around the world to meet our new fellows and ideate solutions to challenging problems. The poem was inspired by having recently read the book *Big World, Small Planet* by Johan Rockström and Mattias Klum, which outlines a brief history of humanity's ascent and introduces Planetary Boundaries theory. Johan was a keynote speaker at the summit that year and the poem served the purpose of introducing him to the stage in a creative and thought-provoking way, while also cheekily announcing my pregnancy to a crowd of many friends and peers. If my performance of "The Water Poem" in Saskatoon had been my first epiphany as to the power of creative storytelling in changing views on social and environmental issues, this one sealed the deal. I was stunned when several grey-haired businessmen came up to me afterwards, each with tears in their eyes, and explained how much my poem had moved them. These were archetypes of the people who have come to represent power and status in the patriarchal, capitalist societies in which we live—hardly the young, liberal arts crowd that I had become accustomed to performing to earlier in my poetry career. Here was something truly powerful; I had taken my poetry from the domain of bar rooms and dusty back rooms in museums, and cut through into the business community on a topic of immense complexity. It helped of course that I had woven in a deeply personal story about the impending arrival of a new life, but the perspective that our current snapshot of humanity represents only a tiny blip in the grand scheme of our species' evolution was one that had clearly hit home. Mulling over the response in the following couple of days, my surprise turned to contemplation of the power of engaging diverse sectors and communities of interest through art, and it was at the end of that conference that I got up on stage and publicly announced my intentions to write this book.

More and more the interconnected nature of humanity began to infiltrate my poetry and storytelling work, as I increasingly moved towards weaving in threads of global change, diverse viewpoints, and a philosophical questioning of what it takes to shift narratives in this day and age. While much of my earlier poetry work was about claiming my voice and honing my identity, the more I learned about the nature of systems change, the more I saw my craft as an opportunity to extend an invitation across sociopolitical boundaries. I began to write poems that aimed to inspire and engage a broad range of people to think about the future in terms of possibility. But knowing what I had learned about the power of personal narratives over abstract descriptions of global issues, the constant challenge I faced was navigating the right balance between drawing on my experiences and ensuring that my story didn't take over.

For centuries the mythic narrative of the hero's journey has been an effective framework for sharing stories of overcoming adversity and transforming the self. It was popularised by Joseph Campbell in the mid-twentieth century, but in reality it has been capturing hearts and minds for generations. If you are unfamiliar with the concept, the story goes something like this: A person, traditionally male, sets out on some sort of physical or metaphorical journey. At first reluctant to leave their comfortable existence, they eventually heed the call to fulfil a quest that they have been tasked with or they set out on a mission to save somebody from imminent doom. Along the way they face many enemies, forces, or situations that are seemingly colluding against their success. Sometimes they are even battling against themselves. They push on through with a little help from a few wise souls, allies, or supernatural powers along the way, go through an initiation process of sorts, often overcome the villain, and learn much about themselves, returning home forever transformed. One of the reasons that the hero's journey is so effective at capturing our imaginations is that it suggests that everyone has it within them to grow and to overcome their fears. In a Western world that adheres to the cult of personality, values individualism, and reveres those who are self-made, the focus of the hero's journey on self-transformation is naturally appealing. It's a story of possibility that plays on our love of tension and the overcoming of adversity. It's the promise that your current circumstances need not define the rest of your life. It's the story of the ne'er-do-well who had a wake-up call and turned his life around. It's the story of the entrepreneur who started out with nothing, and went through many hardships to develop their world-changing idea into a multi-million-dollar company.

There are several reasons I think the traditional hero's journey narrative needs to be approached with care when it comes to the work of solving systemic problems. The first is the same reason that makes it so popular—it focuses on the self. It is linear, narrow, and is fixated on a singular outcome: the transformation of the hero. All other players are secondary to the main storyline of the hero. They inevitably serve some purpose, but almost always to support the objectives of the protagonist. In systems change work, no one has the sole responsibility or indeed capability to single-handedly solve our problems. There are instead hundreds or even thousands of heroes working in the background towards a common goal. If we are to bring each person or group within a system to the table, then each one's journey is important and worthy of a story to be told. Highlighting the story of just one of those people amplifies the narrative of the individual, bestowing special qualities upon them. A spotlight on the work of one person may cast a shadow on another. So the question becomes, who is left in the shadows? How do our biases and prejudices perpetuate predominant narratives of who gets to be a hero and who doesn't? All those side characters, the ones who supplied key support or did the legwork of building relationships with other stakeholders, what of their story?

Secondly, the hero's journey often paints a singular picture of the hero and of the villain. It seldom makes room for the multiplicities of self that make up our lives. We are complex, multi-dimensional creatures, and most of us present subtly different versions of ourselves in different contexts. We adjust our behaviours, body language, levels of engagement, and even manner of speaking depending on the situation. We tell different stories to our childhood friends and college buddies than we do to new clients or colleagues around the water cooler at work. Yet the narrow version of events contained within the typical hero's journey presents only one version of the hero, in a defined context or situation. In part, I think this is due to our propensity for dualistic thinking. Many of us are uncomfortable with paradox and ambiguity. We tend to see things in black and white, wrong and right, good and evil. But truth is seldom a universally accepted thing; in most cases it is subjective. Sometimes multiple, seemingly opposing things are true at once. What happens when the heroine who was so noble on her quest turns out to be an aggressive driver or undermines her coworkers? What happens when the villain redeems himself with a moment of vindication or relatable humanity? As we face intersecting challenges marred by complexity, it is more important than ever to allow for and become more comfortable with paradox and non-linear, non-exclusive stories.

The third reason I find the hero's journey narrative problematic in systems change work is that most often there is an ending. The story has a concise finish to it, as if life stopped at the end of the tale. The subtext is that the hero lives happily ever after, or at least solved their big problem and has a bright future ahead. But life does go on. Short of an inevitably disappointing sequel, there is little scope for us as consumers of a story to find out what happened next in our hero's life. Presuming they didn't die at the end of the story, there is always a next day, or week, or year. What happens then? Does another story begin? Do we see a merging of stories? Do the regaled tales of the hero's journeys and newfound insights serve to change the way their community behaves back home? Despite their almost religious adherence to the hero's journey story arc, one thing that the Marvel and DC superhero franchises do well is to embed the stories of their characters within the context of an ongoing saga. There is an interconnected complexity in the storytelling, with each character being portrayed at one time as the hero in their own story, while other times being cast as an adversary or sidekick in someone else's story. Imagine if we started applying this level of nuance and multiplicity to the ways that we tell and consume stories of people in our lives?

Where I do see the hero's journey being useful in helping us to tackle wicked problems is in coming back to its core message of transformation. Joseph Campbell originally introduced the hero's journey as the "monomyth," implying that deep human truths are contained beneath the individual details. As such it may be apt for these times to apply it through a collective lens. Although not unheard of, it is rare to see the hero's journey model applied to tell the story of the transformation of a community, a group, or an organisation. In the hyper-competitive daily battle for online attention, individual stories have taken over, often at the expense of the family, neighbourhood, or other human social unit. What if we invested more into highlighting the stories of large groups or sectors of society who worked together to transform themselves against the stacked odds? Taking this a step further, what if we were to start telling the story of humanity on its own hero's journey, undergoing a collective global transformation?

The story of EHF is one of a diverse community of over five hundred fellows from some thirty-five countries, applying very different theories of change towards systemic problems and becoming stronger together through the cross-pollination of ideas. EHF is modelled on the natural world—just as a natural ecosystem thrives based on the relationships between many diverse plants, animals, insects, and fungi, so too does a community of change. Together the fellows represent almost any area of impact imaginable, including collaborative finance; regenerative agriculture; play-based education; affordable housing; renewable energy; circular economies; indigenous empowerment; and leading-edge technologies such as AI, blockchain, and immersive virtual and augmented reality. Some were working within traditional company structures, others within social enterprises, not-for-profits, charities, or government organisations. Thanks to the partnership that our team developed with Immigration New Zealand, international fellows gained access to a Global Impact Visa. This purpose-built visa was unique in that it assessed entrepreneurs, investors, and systems change leaders against their perceived potential to create positive impact for New Zealand and the rest of the world, rather than against a standardised set of criteria and boxes to tick. It was a bold and radical experiment, as the first visa programme in the world to place positive impact front and centre. It was a move that not only sought to change narratives underpinning grand global challenges and humanity's ability to solve them, but to counter populist narratives of immigration. Our team was actively trying to shift the immigration story from one focused on additional social pressures and a drain on resources, to a story that highlighted the immense value that immigrants could bring. We wanted to find out what might happen when diverse people from all over the world got together to trial revolutionary new ideas and products in a moderately progressive country with an agile and responsive innovation scene.

In building the EHF community, our team vetted and selected fellow candidates against the values of the organisation, which included authenticity, humility, interconnectedness, and the Māori practice of kaitiakitanga, which loosely translates to "stewardship." In part these values were modelled on the fellowship's namesake Sir Edmund Hillary, a name that we did not carry lightly. New Zealand's most famous son, he is best known for being one of the first two people to summit Mount Everest alongside Tenzing Norgay. But what is less known about Sir Ed (as he is colloquially known in New Zealand) is that he subsequently spent several decades quietly helping to build schools, hospitals, and flight training centres to improve the lives of Sherpa communities in the Himalayas. EHF applicants who clearly displayed large egos were for the most part eliminated in the first round of the selection process. We structured our orientation weeks for new cohorts around our values, and they served as a launch pad for a collective hero's journey of sorts, as fellows had the opportunity to deeply connect and learn about each other's strengths. Each of these individuals had their own story of course, and I loved having the chance to investigate the humans behind the organisations, where they had come from, the details of their journey, and most importantly why they cared about the problem they were trying to solve. In researching their stories, I went to great lengths to dig into what motivated them. I was less interested in the individual ventures or the multi-million-dollar exits, and more in the pivotal moments of their story that were innately human and relatable. Many of these people who were achieving extraordinary things had very ordinary moments peppered throughout their history—a memorable conversation with their grandmother as a young child, the breakdown of a marriage, or a moment of clarity while out in nature. These were the mythic moments I was interested in, the glimpses of truth beneath the noise. They were the undeniable turning points that represented the start of transformation. I wanted the audience to see elements of themselves in the stories and realise that it doesn't take extraordinary talent to develop world-changing ideas, but rather a solid dedication to do so and a driving passion for change. The stories of the individual fellows were powerful but as they came to life and started intersecting, the narrative of the whole community began to emerge. I glimpsed the potential for us to solve complex, global challenges by paying attention to these profound, quiet moments that we each have, and letting them serve as guiding myths towards where we want to go as a global society.

We didn't always succeed at adhering to a collective hero's story. Transcending individual narratives to reorient the story towards one of collective impact and systems change is no small ask. It was particularly difficult for those who were more entrenched in the story of the "heropreneur," which is rife within many tech communities and tends to be elevated in some cultures above others. Some fellows were able to grasp the concepts of interdependence more readily than others, and it is a gradual, long-term task to dismantle traditional narratives of hierarchy that inform relationships and perceived status between investors, entrepreneurs, and those who are more focused on grassroots social action. But by taking a long-term, emergent view of systems change, the threads of separate stories within EHF are weaving together to support a series of new narratives around the ultimate purpose of business, technology, agriculture, society, and the economy.

———

Around the same time as we were developing the fellowship, I connected online with Devi Lockwood, a young woman on a fascinating storytelling journey. She was travelling around the world by bicycle having conversations with strangers with the aim of collecting a thousand and one stories about water and climate change, and was soon to arrive in Wellington. When we arranged to meet at a local cafe, she rocked up on her bike with a tattered cardboard sign around her neck that read: "Tell me a story about water." The flip side encouraged the same for climate change.

Devi's journey began with a memorable Harvard professor of folklore and mythology, Deborah Foster, who helped her to realise that stories serve a function of constantly constructing and changing our identities and narratives of the world:

> I realised that storytelling was all around me. It was in the dinner table conversations I was having with my friends. It was in the things my grandparents talked about at Thanksgiving, when I used to be so frustrated hearing the same stories over and over again. And then I realised that we were constructing our identity as a family unit in real time, and that it had a function in developing our story.

From there she became fascinated with people's stories, and after a knee injury forced her from rowing training into cycling to rebuild her strength, she decided to embark on a 1200-kilometre ride down the Mississippi River Trail during her summer holidays with her bike and a cheap audio recorder. She camped and stayed with friendly strangers who took her in, gathering stories about intensified storms, saltwater encroachment on the land, and people making the decision to leave their small communities as water infrastructure projects in the big cities were leaving them behind. She was hooked on hearing stories, and convinced Harvard to give her a larger grant for what was supposed to be a year of "purposeful wandering" that turned into five. She spent time in the Pacific, talking to people in Fiji and the small island nation of Tuvalu, which with a highest elevation point of just 4.6 metres is at particular risk of rising sea levels. She cycled throughout New

Zealand, Australia, and South-East Asia, and interviewed people in the 400,000-strong crowd at the 2014 People's Climate March in New York. She met climate change deniers along the way of course, and listened to their stories too. Other times she was challenged by climate activists on the carbon miles that she was racking up on her travels by flying, which resulted in some hitched rides around the Pacific on cargo ships and sailboats. When we met in Wellington, I shared with her "The Water Poem" and anecdotes from my self-imposed month of water conservation.

Throughout her travels Devi encountered many variations on similar themes, with each person having their own deeply personal experiences with water. Those that stuck with her the most included the story of a young woman in Tuvalu who had a newborn during a time of drought. She and her husband would wash themselves in the saltwater lagoon to conserve water, but the baby's skin was far too delicate to withstand bathing in salt water. Another time she met a man in Kazakhstan who told her a story he'd never told anyone else before. Growing up in Afghanistan without plumbing in their house, his family would gather water from the river and boil it so it was safe to drink. One day while his parents were out, his young brother got tangled near the fire. The boiling water spilled onto him, burning him badly. He died of his injuries, and the man shared with Devi how he had felt responsible for not watching his brother more closely:

It was clearly a really defining moment in his life, because he felt for the longest time like it was his fault—that if he had done something different, because he was the older brother, that he could have avoided his brother's death. What ended up happening in his life is that he decided to become a water engineer because he said that this shouldn't have to happen to anyone else. He wants to find the solution that's going to get safe water into homes for families throughout Central Asia. That defining narrative of himself, and how he's constructed who he is and what he wants to be in the world, is also clearly a great source of pain. He shared that every time he drinks a glass of water, he thinks about his brother.

Devi feels immensely grateful to have heard so many stories from ordinary people around the world who are being affected by systemic challenges relating to water and climate change, and who are collectively crafting new narratives around how to respond to these challenges. She has written a book, *1,001 Voices on Climate Change*, to share the stories that she gathered on her travels,[1] and now works as a journalist. Devi describes how hearing the stories of all the unsung heroes out there has made her better at both telling and receiving stories:

> It's about just showing up and being fully present, deeply listening, not being distracted, and making eye contact. Being comfortable with silence is a huge part of it; I was very uncomfortable with silence when I started out. Then I started to realise that there's a sort of rhythmic architecture to silence and every type of silence is slightly different. And sometimes you just have to sit with that and be okay with it. I've seen the insides of so many kitchens around the world now. That's where all the best storytelling happens.

The intimacy of these personal stories is what captivates us as social, storytelling beings, and Devi's experience shows how willing people are to tell their stories when given the chance. The more stories we collect, from many different views and perspectives, the more we can start to understand and appreciate that humanity is on a collective hero's journey as we work to address complex challenges together. But we cannot do that without first understanding ourselves and our own stories.

9

EXAMINING OUR STORIES OF SELF

As I entered my final year of primary school at age ten, I had one singular wish: I wanted nothing more than to be a student road warden who helped kids to cross the road at the zebra crossings near our school. I wanted to wear the bright orange vest. I wanted to swing out the big orange signs. I wanted to have the power to stop traffic, and to be seen as the responsible one who was providing a public service. I had been watching older kids doing it for years, and to me it seemed the pinnacle of earned respect. I put my name forward at the beginning of the year, and waited expectantly. When I found out that my application had been declined, I was crushed. The message, relayed through my parents, was that my maturity levels were not high enough to take on this important responsibility. I was seen as too silly, always clowning about. It was a devastating blow, and I was angry and confused. I couldn't understand how the adults would assume that just because I liked to make people laugh and be silly in the schoolyard, that I couldn't also be serious when I needed to be. There was nothing I took more seriously than crossing the road, and so I was surprised to learn that by being silly in situations where it was harmless, that people would assume that I lacked the ability to turn it off and sincerely focus on a task.

This familiar situation played out again in my final year at my all-girls high school, when the school went through the process of selecting the head girl, the deputy, and a group of prefects. Customary in schools across many Commonwealth countries, these leadership roles are inherited from the British school system. Being appointed as one of them meant advocating for students, acting as a liaison between teachers and students, helping new students to settle in, and checking school leave passes at the gates during lunchtime. Because those selected acted as representatives of the student body and the school, the roles hold a fair amount of prestige and responsibility. I had been involved in a lot of extracurricular activities, got pretty good grades, and was for the most part polite and respectful of my teachers. Teachers chose the prefects, while senior students had a say in electing the head girl and deputy. Although I had no expectations nor aspiration to take out either of the top positions, I was surprised when I was once again overlooked for prefect selection. Looking back, it might have had something to do with being caught by the Deputy Principal running down a dorm hallway late at night in a *Scream* mask at our recent school leadership camp. But again, my view was that just because I had an affinity for silliness, it didn't mean that I wasn't prepared to knuckle down and take things seriously when required.

This label of being the Class Clown—indeed those exact words were scrawled across several of my school reports—was an identity I carried with me into the future. Originally defined by innate personality traits, the story of myself as The Clown became one that I lived into partly out of the effect that I saw being funny had in elevating my social status as a young child, partly out of a sense of expectancy, and partly for the sheer fun of it. I just loved telling jokes and making people laugh. Yet when it came down to it being the singular, defining story that others told about me, it became a story laced at times with a sense of shame and not being good enough which I carried into adulthood. It manifested in me always being worried about what others would think, particularly those who were in positions of authority. If I was not one of them, as I had come to understand through these experiences growing up, then I was surely someone who should always defer to them. This influenced everything from my relationship with my parents to the way I would behave in work settings when I believed I didn't have the authority to speak my mind or offer my opinion, lest I be seen as lacking in maturity or experience to properly understand the situation.

The stories we tell about ourselves and that others tell about us ultimately shape us as individuals. As human beings, we generally want to be perceived as rational, consistent beings who are accepted by others, and so we reinforce our stories and behave in alignment with them, further honing our identities. When we tell them enough times, our lives may cease to inform our stories, but rather our stories inform us. They become the yardstick by which we measure ourselves. As has been brought into popular understanding by Brené Brown, overcoming our shame, embracing vulnerability, and having the courage to tell our stories has great potential. When we view vulnerability not as a weakness but rather a great strength, we open the door to more meaningful connection.[1]

Given their power to influence our thinking and behaviour, it is easy to forget that we are not our stories. They influence us greatly, yes, but they do not make up the totality of our identity. They are simply the lenses through which we view ourselves, and sometimes these lenses are faulty. Our memories are on the whole pretty unreliable indicators of the past. Our stories of self may hone in on our shortcomings and if we believe them without question, they can have harmful, limiting effects on our lives. Alternatively, we might tend to minimise the bad and emphasise the good about ourselves and our past, which isn't really ideal or honest either. Thankfully our stories of self are not set in stone. We can choose to reframe them in terms of what we learned, understanding why we behaved in certain ways, and being gentle with ourselves. We can hold up to scrutiny the stories we carry about ourselves, those that inform the very core of our identities. We can examine whether they are mostly positive or negative. Are they supporting us to live our best lives or are they doing us harm? How might somebody else tell our stories, from a different point of view? And what might we learn from the way they tell those stories?

Once we begin to objectively explore our stories in a kind, compassionate, and non-judgmental way, we gain a better understanding of the assumptions and narratives that inform the way we think and act. This work forms the basis of Narrative Therapy, a form of psychotherapy developed in the 1970s and 80s by Australian social worker Michael White and New Zealander David Epston, a family therapist.[2] The practice can help individuals to identify and challenge dominant discourses that are shaping their lives in negative ways. Patients name their stories, distance themselves from them, and pave the way for developing new relationships with them. This model can also be directly applicable to teams, communities, and even whole nations, providing us with the agency to collectively re-author our destinies.[3] On both a personal and collective level, we can embrace the stories that are serving us well and distance ourselves from those that are impeding our growth or reinforcing unhelpful views or habits. We can identify their origins and understand the moments along the way that either have served to challenge or reinforce those stories. Where we find our long-carried stories are doing us a disservice, alternative versions are often just sitting in the background, ready for us to shine a light upon.

The story of myself as The Clown, somewhat tamed from my early years although never fully suppressed, need not be the singular defining story of my life. My other stories of self include that of the Playful Mother, the Spoken Word Artist, the Nature Lover, the Avid Skier, the Fearless Dancer, the Recovering Cynic, and the Ever-Curious Questioner. I've also learned that even when I do decide to be a clown, it's not necessarily a negative thing—my friends appreciate the humour I bring to our gatherings, and we all know the world needs a bit of laughter sometimes.

Many of us think that we don't have good stories or that our stories are not of interest to others. Whoever you are, your stories are legitimate. You are the utmost authority on your own life, and there is value in what you have to share, whatever it may be. Nobody else sees the world through your eyes, with your exact set of lived experiences. What you may consider mundane, irrelevant, ordinary, or inconsequential may be a point of great learning for someone else. I'll never forget the sheer terror of a poetry performance I did once in a friend's living room to about a dozen or so close friends. A few of them had banded together and pitched in for the top-tier pledge on a crowdfunding campaign I ran to fund my trip to Women of the World Poetry Slam in Minneapolis in 2013. The reward at that level was a personal performance at the location of choice. For my friends, that location was in the comfort of their home during a midwinter birthday celebration. Before I began, I stared back at the faces of my friends—people who I loved dearly, people I had shared highs and lows with, people who would support me no matter what. And all I wanted to do was run away and vomit in the bathroom. There was a knot in my stomach and a tightness in my chest. I fumbled my way through the first few poems, visibly shaking, before settling into a groove and beginning to relax a little. It was, still to this day, the hardest performance of my life. But afterwards I felt fantastic and liberated, and one of my friends shared how my poems had made him think about his own life and purpose, and the way he engaged with others to encourage social change.

The learning doesn't stop with others—often we can learn a lot about ourselves by telling our stories. One time performing at a conference I screwed up a poem so badly, forgetting lines and fumbling my way through for several minutes, that I paused and then announced that I was just going to start again. The awkward tension in the room was broken, and the audience broke into hearty applause. The second attempt was a much better performance, and people who were in the audience have since shared with me how refreshing it was to see someone realise they weren't happy with how a story was unfolding, and making the bold decision to just start afresh. It was a lowering of my armour, and a moment of vulnerability that was excruciatingly painful at the time, but it made me more confident than ever in the power of being authentic. Aside from learning not to leave it until the last minute to memorise a new poem, I also learned that it's okay to make mistakes, and that often others will be supportive and forgiving when you choose to own them. The examples I've used here involve public, oral storytelling, but of course not everyone has the opportunity nor desire to tell their stories from the stage. The same learning can occur in much smaller groups or even one-on-one settings. Even when our stories don't come out right and we are uncomfortable, there is an opportunity to learn about ourselves, gain confidence, and further refine how we tell our stories and learn from each other.

There can also be a lot of value in hearing the stories that others tell about you, particularly if you are someone who tends to be your own worst critic. Another person's perspective can be invaluable in helping you to reframe your version of a life event, an interaction, a happening at work, or a long-held narrative you hold about yourself. Of course, the stories that others tell about you aren't always positive or helpful, so we need to learn which ones to take with a grain of salt. The stories that others tell about us are, by their very nature, always narrow or incomplete snapshots of our whole selves. They may be those that Nigerian author Chimamanda Ngozi Adichie refers to in her viral 2009 TED talk as "single stories," and there is a risk that they become a defining narrative of a person. Just like the harmful stories that we craft about ourselves can constrain us, believing all the stories that others tell about us without examining whether or not they hold truth or whether they are helpful to us is a recipe for serious self-doubt. If, however, we find that there is a seed of truth in the stories that others hold about us, they can be of great assistance in self-reflection and personal growth.

A couple of years ago I was writing a story on the innovation scene in Christchurch and specifically about the EHF fellows who had chosen the city as their new home in New Zealand. I had written the bulk of the article and was looking for an interesting hook to open the story. I settled on drawing comparisons between these international innovators and the early Europeans in the Canterbury region, who arrived when the first four ships of English, Irish, and Scottish settlers landed in 1850. I hadn't fully thought it through but was attempting to draw parallels between nineteenth-century voyagers sailing across the world to unfamiliar lands and the modern-day pioneers of new technologies, systems, and ways of thinking that could address big global challenges. Once it was published and shared with the EHF community, it quickly became clear that some of the fellows didn't appreciate being compared to New Zealand's first major wave of colonisers. Looking over what I had written and published, I felt somewhat mortified. I considered myself someone who was pretty aware of the legacy of harm that colonisation has left on these islands. I'm on a continual learning journey for sure, but I thought that I was well on my way. To realise that I had made such an obviously inappropriate and offensive comparison, reinforcing the Eurocentric story of the colonising settlers as brave pioneers and leaving untold the uncomfortable truths surrounding the theft of land and coercion over local Māori communities, made me want to crawl into a hole. I unpublished the article and rewrote the opening, and then spent the next few days wondering how I had made such an obvious mistake. It did not fit in with who I thought I was, and it was not a narrative that I thought was in line with my identity. Except that it was.

I came to realise that the story of those four ships was indeed intricately woven into my personal identity. One line of my mother's family on her father's side emigrated to New Zealand on one of those ships. From an early age I had heard the stories, spoken with pride, of how the family of eight had travelled across from England on third-class tickets on the *Cressy*; the father a shepherd, the mother the bearer of six children aged 10, 8, 6, 4, 2, and infant. As a child, I would read their names etched into a plaque in Christchurch's Cathedral Square, tracing my fingers over the etchings in the cold metal and imagining the months-long sea voyage with six young children. I wondered what sort of life they had lived before and why they had chosen to undertake such a journey. I heard how they had spent several months living in a tin shack in the port town of

Lyttelton before making the journey over the Port Hills to settle on the fertile Canterbury Plains just north of Christchurch.

What I realised in those few days of reflection was that despite learning a fair amount about colonisation and the New Zealand Wars, I had yet to reconcile the story of that part of my heritage with the new information I had been receiving. I had understood on some level that the European colonisation of Aotearoa (the Māori name for New Zealand) had seen the systemic crushing of Māori sovereignty and blatant disregard for te Tiriti o Waitangi (the Treaty of Waitangi) that the Crown of England had signed with more than five hundred Māori rangatira (chiefs) in 1840. I knew that it was not a part of our history that I felt particularly good about. But I had yet to do the deep, personal work of closely examining the story of my ancestors that I had been told my whole life, and questioning the legitimacy and legacy of that narrative. I hadn't taken the time to understand how my perpetuation of that story was contributing towards the effects of colonisation that are still very much alive in Aotearoa New Zealand today. I had yet to shed the pride I had felt from an early age at my family being amongst the first Europeans to come. I still held the narrative of them as brave adventurers, ready to abandon all that they knew in favour of an unknown life. The problem is not so much that that narrative didn't hold truth, but rather that it was incomplete and one-sided. My ancestors weren't exactly the epitome of the landed gentry; they were just poor shepherds looking to escape the brutally oppressive British class system and have a better shot at life. They were possibly quite naive about the extent to which land around the country was being confiscated from Māori communities. But their naivety and prior history of oppression doesn't change the fact that they were also colonisers who later gained much at the cost of great harm to the Indigenous people of this land. Long before there were those four ships, there were seven pioneering waka—canoes used by early Māori navigators to reach Aotearoa New Zealand. Both stories are true, but one has been dominating the history that is taught in our classrooms much more than the other. For me, it is hard but ultimately necessary work to try to reconcile them, or at least to recognise how much the story has been skewed for close to two hundred years. I am grateful to those who spoke up when I first published that story and pointed out the problematic aspects of the narrative, as they provided me with an important lesson in my storytelling journey.

Many of our stories of self begin long before we are born. They are the stories of our ancestors and the stories of our culture, passed down from generation to generation. Some are clear, tangible, and repeated often enough to become family legend or national folklore; others are invisible, inherited accounts of the past that guide our assumptions and identities. We inherit intergenerational triumphs and traumas, many of which we are completely oblivious to, and our lives may turn out very differently depending on which of these feature more prominently in our ancestral histories. If we are to look back twelve generations, which is only three hundred years or so, each of us has 4096 ancestors. That's a lot of stories passed down through the ages. A lot of triumph and a lot of trauma. They are the stories that are embedded into the foundations of our identities and our culture. They influence the way we have built our societies, and whose stories get heard and whose don't. They influence which stories we tell about ourselves, and which ones we tell about others. Some of these stories are incredibly helpful, acting as anchoring myths that guide us on our path while others continue to perpetuate harm. While we can't change the past, we can choose to acknowledge these latter types of stories and the harm that they cause, and seek to understand alternative narratives. We can change the way we tell them, who the heroes are, who the villains are, what happened, and how it happened. These are subjective elements to a story that change depending on who is telling it. We may even discover that there are no heroes or villains, just people.

The story of my ancestors making the three-month sailing from England is still part of my story. It always will be, but that doesn't mean it should be a story that I hold up without scrutiny, without careful and humble investigation. I did not engage personally in the colonisation of this land, but I do continue to reap the benefits of it at the ongoing cost to Māori, many of whom have instead inherited generations of trauma, the suppression of their language and culture, the theft of their land, and raids upon their communities by settlers and Crown troops alike. While I cannot change the past, I can act in the present and in the future to help shed light on the stories that have been hidden from popular culture for so long. Not necessarily to tell these stories, as they are not mine to tell— they are the stories of Ngāi Tahu, the iwi with sovereignty over Ōtautahi, the place that was renamed Christchurch. But I can elevate the voices of those who they belong to, read other accounts of the settling of the region, and learn the histories of Ngāi Tahu as told by themselves. I can constantly examine my stories of self and decide whether they still ring true for me, or if they have shifted.

Human beings are not benign entities, experiencing life in a passive way. We are informed and influenced by the world around us, and in turn we are influencing the world. We are constantly becoming, yet our changes are not always celebrated. In politics and business, for example, changing your story or perspective on something may be viewed as a U-turn and has come to symbolise flakiness, unsteadiness, untrustworthiness, and being unfit to lead. But quite the opposite is true. It takes a great deal of self-reflection and careful examination (and particularly in the case of politicians, a great deal of courage) to look back into the depths of your past, and realise that the narratives and stories that were driving you no longer ring true. What once felt so passionate and alive for you may no longer bring the same degree of satisfaction or assuredness that the path you are on is the right one. As we evolve, so too do our stories. It's worth remembering as we navigate our way through this life, and we could do well to afford others the same patience and grace that we would hope to receive ourselves as our stories continue to unfold and evolve.

10

THE STORY CIRCLE GOES DIGITAL

In mid-March 2020, I had tickets to see one of my favourite musicians, Amanda Palmer, perform in St Peter's church in Wellington on a Monday night. It had been a number of years since Amanda was last in New Zealand, and she had since given birth to a son who was around the same age as my own. A deviation from some of her previous raucous theatrics in darkened venues, this evening was set to be a night of raw, honest storytelling in what Amanda promised would be her most human and vulnerable stage-show to date. In the previous week, however, the global situation with COVID-19 had taken on a new level of gravity. Amanda had entered New Zealand the day before mandatory self-isolation for new arrivals came into place, along with her son and her husband, fantasy writer Neil Gaiman. Given that Wellington had just had its first confirmed case of the virus and several other countries were already in complete lockdown, Amanda made the last-minute decision to cancel what would have been the final show on her eighty-one-show world tour. Always the creative thinker, she opted instead for a free global webcast from inside the church. It was a strange feeling to be watching it that evening from the comfort of my own living room, knowing that it was being broadcast from just a couple of kilometres down the road.

As she is renowned for doing, Amanda asked her audience for help at one point, inquiring if anyone in Wellington had a copy of the classic children's book *Goodnight Moon* that they could drop off. I rummaged amongst our jumbled mess of kids' books and toys to find our copy, and drove quickly down to the church banging loudly on a side door until they let me in. Then in a surreal sense of wonder, I settled into a church pew to watch as Amanda and Neil sang, read, and chatted about the strangeness and uneasiness of it all to a global audience via a laptop camera. In a scene steeped in dark irony, Neil read out passages from Edgar Allan Poe's Gothic short story *Masque of the Red Death*, which is about a group of nobles sheltering in an abbey to avoid a plague. At the close of the show, I sat cross-legged on the floor in a small circle with Amanda and a handful of other people who had found their way into the church, and we all held hands as Neil read us a bedtime story —*Goodnight Moon*. It was magical and wondrous and deeply unsettling all at once. The scene combined the ancient intimacy of a small group sharing stories in a beautiful old wooden church, with a much wider sense of unity and solidarity with thousands of anxious and scared people, who were able to join in courtesy of online telecommunications technology. It was the story circle gone digital. It felt like the beginning of something really significant and in hindsight, it was. For myself and for many others around New Zealand, it was the night that COVID-19 got real.

The ways in which we create, consume, and understand stories is undergoing phenomenal changes. The nature of those stories is in flux, the authors are many, and the ways in which we relate to story is evolving at a rapid pace. For the bulk of humanity's existence, before written language emerged a little over five thousand years ago, storytellers had only two choices: to share their stories through the oral tradition or scribble them out in crude drawings. By contrast, today's choices of medium represent a dizzying blend of the visual, the technological, the interactive, and the poetic. Film and video paint a definitive picture where once we relied solely on imagination. Neatly drawn line graphs and scatter plots have been replaced by beautifully presented infographics and data visualisations. Trans-media storytelling allows stories that begin in one particular place or medium to be transferred and continued in a different medium through online connectivity. There is even scope for online stories to progress offline. In the world of MMORPGs (massively multiplayer online role-playing games), stories and experiences that for the most part are unfolding online are further refined by real-life, in-person meetups where allegiances may change, new partnerships formed, or coups planned. Stories need not even be linear any more, as interactive storytelling introduces multiple protagonists and storylines. From the choose-your-own-adventure type programming that Netflix is experimenting with, to in-depth online stories that combine text, imagery, moving graphics, data, infographics, and video content, interactive stories hand over the reins to whomever is consuming them.

With these changes, everybody and anybody with an internet connection becomes a storyteller, sharing information, thoughts, perspectives, and ideas online. Every day, billions of micro-stories are shared on social media, and there are dozens of tutorials out there that teach users how to develop the perfect Instagram or TikTok video that follows a short but formulaic story arc. The ability of anyone to share their stories widely has done some incredible things in terms of connecting us globally, but it has also inevitably done much damage. Anyone with an agenda, however nefarious, now has a platform to spread their message. Consequently, the proliferation of hate speech, xenophobia, and fake news has blown out to epidemic proportions. And as the technology improves, the potential for misuse rises. Technology has emerged in recent years to create deepfake video content, which uses artificial intelligence (AI) to synthesise remarkably convincing fake video of known figures saying whatever it is the creator wants them to say. Famous examples include footage of former US President Richard Nixon announcing to the world that the 1969 moon landing mission ended in disaster, Facebook CEO Mark Zuckerberg telling us "whoever controls the data controls the future," and a scene from the 90s hit television show *Friends* where each cast member features the face of Nicolas Cage. Microsoft's AI chatbot Tay made headlines in 2016 when its Twitter account start spewing out racist, sexist, anti-Semitic, and sexually charged tweets within twenty-four hours of launching. What happened? The bot, which was modelled on a fun-loving nineteen-year-old woman, learned from its followers—many of whom immediately began trolling it. AI learns from humans, and so along with the useful information we want it to learn, it also picks up our biases, our prejudices, our assumptions, and our narratives about how the world is. Technology itself is agnostic of course; it is how we develop it and what we do with it that makes the difference. Whether it is AI, the Internet of Things, biotechnology, robotics, drones, or 3D printing, the conversations around how to ethically develop technology without further entrenching systemic injustices, seem starkly secondary to the buzz surrounding the technologies themselves. I question how much more technology we really need to solve our biggest problems; to me, it appears that it's our cultural and social systems that most need to change.

The good news is that just as technology can be used to spread hate and false information, it can be used to strategically tell stories that inspire and activate humanity to do good. While much of the investment into Virtual and Augmented Reality (VR/AR) has gone into the entertainment and gaming sector so far, these technologies are showing a lot of promise in treating subjects with mental health issues such as Post Traumatic Stress Disorder (PTSD). The ability for VR/AR to trigger an empathetic response has massive implications for sectors like international aid or in helping people to understand the real and tangible effects of climate change. As we begin to see the addition of scent profiles and haptic feedback technologies that activate our sense of touch, the immersive experience will become even closer to reality. Imagine the experience of being virtually immersed in the Brazilian rainforest during a clear-felling event, smelling the burning of chainsaw upon wood, feeling the heat on your face as scrub is burned, and hearing the trees crashing around you as birds and other wildlife flee for their lives. Or imagine the compassion and connection you might feel if the scene placed you within a refugee camp, with the stench of cramped bodies, the wailing of children, and the cold touch of concrete-floored cages. Such experiences could help us immensely to relate deeply to the experiences of people across the world. Matched with clever storytelling and clear data about our consumer choices, such experiences could lead to significant changes in behaviour towards a more sustainable and just global society.

Topaz Adizes is a man on a mission to connect humanity by redefining how we interact with stories in the documentary form. I first met him, an energetic and fast-paced talker with a thick New York accent and a sizeable appetite for caffeine, as he bounded off a bus at a retreat centre a little south of Auckland to attend the Edmund Hillary Fellowship's inaugural cohort orientation week. Having only met on a video call on a couple of occasions, he enveloped me in a giant bear hug before immediately launching into deep discussions around the future of storytelling. Topaz and the team at his studio The Skin Deep won an Emmy Award in 2015 for their interactive documentary *{THE AND}*. An online experience that begins by asking viewers a few short questions, *{THE AND}* custom-curates a short documentary featuring intimate conversations between lovers, siblings, children, parents, friends, ex-partners, and any other kind of relationship pairing. Filmed with two individuals sitting facing each other and drawing cards in turn to ask each other probing and sometimes deeply challenging questions, the interactions make for extremely addictive viewing, as you are invited as a voyeur into the most vulnerable and intimate conversations between people.

Topaz created The Skin Deep to produce experiences that explore human connection, and he saw conversations between people in *{THE AND}* as a vehicle for that:

> I wanted to see if I could illuminate the space between, and by that I mean the space that's between two people that are in relationship, which is alluded to by the title of the project. It's not you or me, us or them; it's you and me, us and them.

Topaz has seen a multitude of different ways that people connect with one another and finds joy in the ability of the conversations he films to help define and sometimes even redefine relationships. In that regard, he considers himself less of a storyteller, and more of a story-breaker who is helping to shift narratives around human connection:

Let's say that you assume that love is full of jealousy. You watch *{THE AND}* and you get a glimpse into someone else's relationship, and oh my god, they don't have jealousy. You're witnessing other people's reality and it makes you think that maybe this thesis you have, it's not necessarily a truth. It's just a story. There are as many stories out there and configurations of relationships as there are grains of sand on the beach. We've filmed around a thousand conversations now, and everyone has a different story that rings true for them.

I've witnessed the live experience of *{THE AND}* being filmed on several occasions, with close-up facial shots of each participant broadcast onto large TV screens behind them, and I can tell you that it is equal parts beautiful and uncomfortable. You can watch every emotion play out on the faces of those asking and answering personal questions, and in that moment, there is no hiding of a person's own personal truth. Their faces tell the story half the time without them having to say anything. Inspired by glimpses of humanity and connection, Topaz has grand plans to scale his work to create what he calls "the Wikipedia of human relationships":

The fundamental technology of *{THE AND}* is the question. Modern civilisation is so focused on results or answers. We often forget to look at the questions, and I think that's a more profound place to look for solutions. Imagine if you could go online and type in any kind of relationship or family problem you're having, or search for the kinds of stories you want to hear, and boom, here's five different conversations with people navigating those same messy, human challenges. It's shocking how something so simple can be so profound and cathartic. We're just asking questions.

Each time I find myself in the depth of a *{THE AND}* binge on YouTube, it strikes me that that this sort of stark authenticity and a willingness to deeply listen is key to solving global challenges, particularly when we are dealing with such a diversity of values and cultural differences. This technology is helping me to understand, in all their vulnerable, raw honesty, the strengths of other people's stories and how much influence they have over their lives. I can't help but be empathetic towards people who I have only just been introduced to. It's a potent tonic for a world full of fear, suspicion, and divisive rhetoric. On the state of online media and its role in driving polarisation, Topaz doesn't mince his words:

No one's hearing each other right now. They're shouting to their chorus about somebody else without ever engaging with the other people and actually speaking to them. We now live in a world of post-truth, where everything is a story. The question is can you get people to buy into your myth, your narrative, your story? And are your stories helpful in terms of solving the problems that the world needs to solve? Or are they unhelpful? That's all that matters. We are at this unique time in history where I think everyone's losing their mind, and I just hope we find our hearts in the process.

THE SHIFTING SANDS OF NARRATIVE

POETIC INTERLUDE 3

A CURE FOR THEM

Watch a video of this poem

If we are to believe the stories that dominate our social
    media feed,
there are an evil group of people out there
who are out to destroy our lives.

They do not share our values,
they have no common sense,
they will take away your freedom, bombard you with
    fake news.
Brainwashing your children with their propaganda,
they will do everything in their power

to take away all that you hold sacred.

Beware, they are out there,
the people we call
"Them"

Them, the enemy,
them, those other ones,
them, the ones we must overcome,
the target of every comment section,
everywhere

So confident are we
that we are the ones who are right,
we have turned respectful public debate
into millions of miniature, individual dictatorships of
     the mind.
The teeth of our savage sound bites grow ever sharper
     by the day
while indignant ears remain deaf to anything
that does not reinforce our worldview.

There is no room for reason in a lynch mob,
no longer a gift in give and take.
No space for context and complexity in a 280-character
     tweet.
The air is growing thin in this here echo chamber,
it's getting harder and harder to breathe.

We need not even look too far before we can identify a
     "them."
Even amongst brothers and sisters in arms,
sibling rivalry cuts deep.

The climate activist questions the urgency of queer
       rights if we have no habitable planet to call our
       home.
The unionist challenges foreign aid when a working
       wage can't even feed our own people.
We hear, it's the immigrants who are the problem,
or those people in SUVs.
It's the dairy farmers, the greenies, the feminists, the
       TERFs,
the bankers, the church, the NRA.
It's corporate welfare, guerrilla warfare,
it's the liberal media, the gay agenda,
it's them,
it's they,
it's those people,
if only they would ... Stop!

Listen.
Can you hear that?

That is the sound of singular stories.
It's the sound of petty distractions.
It's the sound of red herrings gasping for breath
as the future slips away.

Oblivious to our own hypocrisy and wasting our
       precious energy,
we are setting ourselves on fire in the hopes that
they will die of smoke inhalation.

It need not be this way.
We can be better than this.
We have the cure for "them,"
it's simple.

It is us.

What if we took our pointing fingers, and we turned
     them upside down
to extend the gentle hand of compromise?
Offered up our gifts and contributions with open hearts,
embracing grace and humility?

That's not to say that we should deny the role of
     privilege,
ignore the wounds from the past,
or cease to pursue our passion for change.
After all, even the Buddha taught non-violence, not
     pacifism.
But let us dismantle systems of oppression
without creating carbon copies addressed to "them."

Step away from the militancy you have held so close,
as a lover.
Soften your heart and walk a mile in shoes that do
     not fit,
shoes that cause you discomfort,
blisters edging their way in
beneath the soles of the feet you have so firmly planted
in the arguments you have convinced yourself are solid.
This place is familiar, it is comfortable.
But we desperately need to stand upon
common ground.

For it is there that we can pinpoint the underlying
     causes
behind our addiction to outrage.
Feelings of grief, of losing that which we hold dear.
Feelings of fear, of those who we do not understand.

Feelings of pain, of leaning into the despair of not
        knowing
how the hell we are going to
get ourselves out of this mess.

Respect the collective wisdom that comes from listening
to many voices that are different from your own.
Find your passion,
and then you do you, and do it well,
while simultaneously seeking to understand
why it is that they care so much about something else.

According to particle physics,
we exchange 98 percent of the atoms in our bodies
with the world around us every year.

So I am you,
and you are me.
And they are us.
And we are them.

We are them.
We are them.
To somebody, somewhere,
you are them.

———

*To view the video of this poem, follow the link below or scan the QR
code at the beginning of the poem.*

alinasiegfried.com/a-cure-for-them

11

THEY ARE US

I FIRST PERFORMED THE POEM "A CURE FOR THEM" AT AN Edmund Hillary Fellowship (EHF) summit of impact-driven leaders from around the world in mid-March 2019. Two days later and some 300 kilometres to the south, a lone gunman with several semi-automatic weapons walked into first one, and then a second mosque in Christchurch, New Zealand. Timing his attack during busy Friday prayers, he calmly and methodically opened fire claiming the lives of fifty-one people, and injuring many more. He had earlier that day published a seventy-four-page manifesto detailing his white supremacist motivations on an online message board, and livestreamed the entire attack on Facebook.

In the wake of the tragedy, New Zealanders went first into a state of shock before rapidly rallying around the Muslim community in an outpouring of grief and support. People from all walks of life flocked to mosques around the country, laying flowers, cards, and teddy bears. Colourful chalked messages of love and solidarity adorned the pavements and shops ran out of flowers. Feeling helpless to do anything of tangible action, my wife and I took our two children down to our local mosque in Wellington. We shed tears, hugged strangers, and looked around at each other, trying to make sense of the surreal and unsettling situation. I held a Muslim boy of about fourteen in my arms as he shook with grief. New Zealand's Prime Minister Jacinda Ardern flew immediately to Christchurch, and her reaction in the following days would trigger both a national and global conversation around our response to acts of terrorism. Rather than focusing on the gunman, her message was one of hope, love, unity, and compassion and that this wasn't the New Zealand that she knew. Her addresses in the following days barely referred to the attacker at all. Speaking in Parliament she urged, "Speak the names of those who were lost rather than the name of the man who took them. He may have sought notoriety but we in New Zealand will give him nothing, not even his name." The media followed suit by agreeing not to publish the gunman's name or image of his face. Ardern's calls for empathy and compassion were matched by her actions. A photo of her hugging a Muslim woman went viral around the world, her face a picture of grief with tightly closed eyes. The image was projected onto the world's tallest building, the 829-metre Burj Khalifa in Dubai, accompanied by the word *salam* and its English translation, "peace."

I watched the news clips in eerie reflection as our prime minister uttered the very same closing words from the poem I had performed two days earlier, "they are us." She used these words in reference to the Muslim community, inferring that an attack on them was an attack on all New Zealanders. In the face of hatred and bigotry, she chose not to engage in us-vs-them rhetoric, but instead adopted a frame of unity. Prime Minister Ardern's response to the man who carried out this heinous act was to take the fuel out of his fundamentalist narrative and focus on the victims and their families, allowing space for mourning and grief. It was a fitting response to unite a nation, and she was awarded accolades from around the world.

The day after the attacks, Ardern signalled sweeping changes to gun laws, which for the most part were welcomed by the public. Social media feeds were full of New Zealanders questioning why anyone would legitimately need semi-automatic weapons, and others expressed surprise that they weren't already banned. There was some pushback from gun lobby organisations and libertarian groups who were concerned about the pace of change, but even the country's largest hunting and fishing group, Fish & Game New Zealand, supported the changes. Within a month the New Zealand Parliament passed a law banning military-style semi-automatic guns and assault rifles.

In part, it was the weight of the shifting public narrative that supported the government to be able to make such drastic changes in such a short period of time. The March 15 attacks were New Zealand's first major case of racially driven terrorism by its modern definition. Many New Zealanders had previously believed, at least on some kind of subconscious level, that this could never happen in little old New Zealand, that somehow we were immune to these sorts of ideologically driven atrocities. This was simply not in line with our long-held national narrative of an egalitarian, multicultural society, where people looked out for each other and lived in relative harmony. It was not who we told ourselves we were. Yes, we had our problems, but tucked away at the bottom of the world we read the headlines from overseas and felt lucky to be shielded away from the woes that other countries faced. I believe it was no accident that the Australian-born shooter chose New Zealand in which to conduct his deadly attack. I think he chose a secular, socially progressive society precisely because it would disrupt the predominant narrative of New Zealand as a safe, tolerant country and send a message to Muslims around the world that they were not safe anywhere.

What this man did not count on was the response of a nation in the following days. The level of support for the Muslim community was widespread, and there was a dogged determination not to let this person direct the story. Instead, stories emerged of those who had acted in service of others. We heard the story of a grandfather who was killed as he threw himself in front of another worshipper to shield them from gunfire. One man had tackled the gunman and knocked him momentarily off his feet, while another threw a portable EFTPOS bank-card reader at his head. The following Friday, members of some of New Zealand's most notorious gangs stood guard outside mosques around the country so that Muslims could come to pray in peace and safety. Outside one mosque, members of a gang thanked the New Zealand police force for their response before performing a powerful haka, a ceremonial Māori dance used to welcome, challenge, support, or pay respect. Imagine how extraordinary that is for a minute, members of a gang thanking the police. Within two days of the shooting, over NZ$10 million was donated for the victims and their families, illustrating the power of the public response when we are moved by a story that so deeply shifts our collective narrative.

In the following weeks and months after the media attention had quietened down, many New Zealanders began a period of intense soul searching and started asking ourselves questions. What exactly had happened here? How could it have happened? And most importantly, why? It kicked off a national dialogue highlighting that New Zealand is in truth not a safe place for many of our people and has not been for a long time. The story of our nation as a tolerant and egalitarian society was an outdated one, or perhaps it had never been true in the first place. The choice of the prime minister's use of the phrase "they are us" was put into question—what did that mean exactly? Who was "us"? I suspect she intended it to be a mark of solidarity suggesting that Kiwis are united as one, but does that really ring true when we look below the surface? Racial profiling, the rise of the alt-right, and more insidious microaggressions are a daily reality for many minorities within our population. Muslims in Christchurch had been warning of the fear of an attack on their community for at least five years before the March 15 shootings, and they expressed anger and frustration that they had not been listened to or taken seriously. A Royal Commission Inquiry report released about a year and half later found that the predominant narrative of Muslims as the perpetrators of terror attacks rather than the victims had deeply infiltrated New Zealand's intelligence agencies, and that they had not been paying adequate attention to the rising threat of the alt-right and white supremacy movements. More widely, the livestreamed attacks lent weight to the global conversation around how technologies that were originally intended to connect us are increasingly doing the opposite. This was the world's first major terror attack to be streamed live on the internet, and it took Facebook twenty-nine minutes to remove the livestream. A further 1.2 million copies of the video were uploaded and subsequently removed from Facebook in the first twenty-four hours. It was us vs them fundamentalism gone viral, and many of us questioned where we go to from here.

12

MOVING BEYOND COPS AND ROBBERS

IMAGINE IF WHEN YOU SIGNED UP TO FACEBOOK OR ANY OTHER social media platform, you were presented with the question of who you wanted to hear from? You could choose to only hear from those who expressed similar views as you, have a balanced feed with a mix of content from those who think like you and those who don't, or have some sort of a "Challenge me" option that provided you with a high proportion of content that would push your buttons and encourage you to see perspectives very different from your own. Which would you choose? For those that chose the extreme diversity of thought option, do you think it would result in people being less dogmatic in their views and embracing opportunities for growth, or would it inevitably descend into a keyboard battlefield of name-calling, blame, and self-righteousness?

Since childhood, many of us have learned that there are good guys and there are bad guys. We learn that peace, prosperity, and happiness is achieved by defeating some foe. Evil will be overcome, the good guys will be heralded as heroes, and the innocent can rest easy once more. At just three years old my son already had 100 percent confidence in the inherent truth of this hero vs villain story. He could tell me in unequivocal terms who was the goodie and who was the baddie in popular television shows. Our efforts to limit his exposure to shows that relied on these narratives and instead encourage cartoons that highlighted community, learning, and the importance of working together, were derailed by his social environment. As rapidly as we could vet shows and avoid them, he picked up equally as many hero vs villain narratives at preschool from other kids. This powerful narrative has infiltrated our lives so deeply that we cannot see others who we disagree with as anything but wrong. We are naturally the hero of our story, and as such we are trained from an early age to identify a villain. I recall one day as a young child in primary school when I couldn't find my pencil, automatically drawing a conclusion and announcing to the teacher, "Someone took my pencil!" I can still see her kind yet steady face as she patiently looked directly at me, and asked, "You mean you can't find your pencil? Let's look for it together, shall we?"

As adults, we are probably pretty unlikely to consciously label heroes and villains in our life. Instead that same mindset manifests itself as *us-vs-them* thinking, also known as *othering*. From workplace grievances and family conflicts to major disagreements between nations or political factions, we pin problems on a real or imagined "other." Searching for simplistic answers to complex problems, we tend to search for a person, community, group, or archetype to blame rather than trying to identify the root causes of a problem or examining our long-held assumptions. Othering sees us reducing a complex, dynamic person or group to a singular story or stereotype. We then focus on that singular narrative and fail to take into account the totality of their human experience. Often these pervasive narratives are inherited, collective grievances passed down through the ages by tribes, nations, and families. That thing that happened once upon a time becomes the defining story of that other group of people or of that other nation. From historic witch trials and religiously driven crusades to genocide that is ongoing today, othering has resulted in unspeakable horrors being inflicted upon people and communities. Today it is exacerbated by obscure pockets of the internet dedicated to highly specific communities of interest and social media algorithms that serve to reinforce what we already believe. Where once people harbouring the seeds of extremist views were tempered by the influence of more moderate members of their community, they can now hide away behind a keyboard and avoid those people entirely, engaging only with those who hold similarly extreme views. In part, this is how fundamentalist extremism breeds.

Historically, othering had an important function. Scarcity of resources in prehistoric times meant that knowing who was part of your group and who wasn't was a matter of survival. During the cold winters, more for you meant less for me. Finding and defending a cave to live in might mean the difference between your clan living on to become ancestors or dying off to be forgotten forever. In today's world, that level of tribalism is seldom required for survival. We have learned how to build shelters and we have the knowledge and ability to grow abundant food (although it should be noted that geopolitical and neo-liberal economic policies put significant brakes on the distribution of that knowledge and food). But we still have that biological hangover that urges us to scan for difference in the people we meet, focusing on what sets them apart, and we align ourselves with those who are like us. That's not to say that tribalism or wanting to nurture a sense of belonging is inherently a bad thing. Collective wisdom, knowledge-sharing, and collaborative culture has done incredible things for humankind. For example, the open source software movement that has provided great leaps in efficiency and productivity, is centred around a certain kind of tribalism that values open collaboration with strangers. Our innate sense of belonging is nurtured by interacting with those who we feel an affinity with. Our great mistake is to believe that the voices that we choose to surround ourselves with are representative of our human nature.

My earlier days of environmental activism were very much informed by an us-vs-them mindset, and I have certainly been guilty of othering people and simplifying a complex situation when I did not agree with someone. My passion for our natural world combined with the steadfast certainty of ideals that comes with youth meant that I felt confident that I was on "the right side." I got involved in almost every environmental movement that came along, attending every protest, taking part in direct actions, and organising petitions. But after a while I began to become uncomfortable with the dogmatic nature of much of the action. I began to realise that I was surrounded by people who were often more interested in being right and being seen to be up on a moral high horse than actually engaging in a constructive dialogue. And then I realised, to my great surprise, that not only was I surrounded by those people, I *was* one of those people. I looked back at what I had achieved, and while there were certainly some individual campaign wins, so many of the underlying problems had been left unchecked. What I had failed to grasp as a passionate young activist is that divisive tactics and finger pointing seldom work to sway people who think differently. They are in fact counter-productive and can serve to only make people dig their heels in deeper.

For all its silliness, the original *Austin Powers* movie features a poignant moment following the death of an anonymous henchman by steamroller. There is a scene immediately afterwards in which the henchman's wife receives the phone call notifying her that he has been killed. Pulling her son in close, she utters the words, "People never think how things affect the family of a henchman." It is, of course, a scene steeped in comedic irony and meant in jest, but therein lies an important lesson in this touching scene: people are multi-dimensional. Henchmen have families. Bad guys are capable of loving, and of being loved. The vast majority of people in the world would consider someone who shoots up a mosque, a church, a school, or a gay nightclub to be a villain driven by evil and hate. Yet in some circles, the people who commit these heinous acts are heralded as heroes. In their narrative of the world and their place within it, they often truly believe that they are doing the world a great good. While the world sees them as evil, it is often their own skewed perception of evil and their desire to rid the world of it, that drives their actions. The same mentality drives all kinds of extremist fundamentalism, whatever the particular type. Let me be explicitly clear at this point that I am not defending or excusing the beliefs and actions of those who display hate and commit violence against people based on their religion, sexual orientation, gender identity, country of birth, or colour of their skin. I deplore their actions and it saddens me deeply that people are driven so strongly to do such things. But seeking to understand how someone came to hold those beliefs does not mean that we agree with them or condone their actions. It is rather an exercise in examining the stories and narratives that drive their beliefs and behaviours, in order to understand the root causes of their worldview. If a part of your body is sick, you would want to learn about that sickness and do what you can to address it. Similarly, I believe the human race is collectively suffering from a deep-seated sickness that stems from othering, and, for myself, I want to better understand it.

What are the consequences of not knowing or understanding each other? The adversarial state of our political systems and online dialogue is one consequence, with both politicians and keyboard warriors trading insults on any number of divisive issues. An extreme consequence is the more overt forms of violence and terrorism such as the mosque shootings in Christchurch. Whatever the form, it stems from the same mindset of dehumanisation of the other. This dehumanisation goes both ways, particularly when someone engages in such a terrible act. It is much, much easier to write someone off as a hateful homophobe, racist, white supremacist, neo-nazi, or general horrible person, than to try to get inside the head of someone who is prepared to gun down a group of strangers, and attempt to understand their story. To do so takes a great deal of courage, self-awareness, and even empathy. It is deeply uncomfortable, counter-intuitive, and may feel like a betrayal to our values and moral code. But by hurling insults, labelling them as evil or terrible, what do we achieve? What do we learn about how those people came to think the way that they do? How do we walk the razor-thin line between standing up and saying that a person did a deplorable thing, while trying to understand and address the underlying causes that drove their actions? Let me also add here that I am writing from the perspective of an educated, cisgendered, white woman from a comfortable, middle-class background, and this grants me an enormous amount of privilege and emotional capacity to dissect these complexities. I do not carry the same collective and individual traumas that people of colour or ethnic minorities do. I have never been on the receiving end of overtly hateful discrimination. Even as a gay woman, my "feminine" or "straight-presenting" appearance to date means that many strangers presume me to be heterosexual, and as such I am afforded that additional privilege when compared to others in the queer community. I recognise that I can never truly understand from a personal standpoint how difficult it might be for others to move beyond both inherited and lived trauma, and seek to understand the people who direct hate at them with such venom.

What I do know is that the world is becoming more polarised by the day, and that to address complex, systemic, global challenges, we need to come together. Dror Moreh's 2012 documentary, *The Gatekeepers*, drew critical acclaim by bringing together the six living former heads of Israeli internal security service Shin Bet. Delving into topics such as the efficacy of torture, the morality of targeted assassination, and the tragedy of collateral damage, the film is often self-reflective in nature. The former head of Shin Bet from 1980 to 1986, Avraham Shalom is quoted on the importance of dialogue to overcome conflict: "Things get clarified. I see you don't eat glass. He sees I don't drink petrol. That's how it is." The Israel-Palestine conflict is incredibly complex and far from resolved, but Shalom's words still hold truth and serve as an important lesson.

To understand a person's way of thinking and the conditions through which extreme views come about, my suspicion is that we need to get a whole lot better at hearing and understanding the stories of those who think differently from us. We need to stop "othering" so much and instead focus on belonging. It's worth noting that when I refer to other people's stories, I mean the personal experiences, anecdotes, and values that inform their beliefs and actions and that hold truth for them. I'm not referring to the "stories" that underpin misinformation and disinformation. Our own stories and personal narratives are subjective—we all apply our own framing and spin on things. But when those in positions of power, whether through democratic election, dictatorship, or by simply having access to an online pedestal and a decent following, invent stories that have no grounding in truth whatsoever, we are talking about a different kettle of fish entirely. Disinformation comes from a place of fear and a desire to control. Diverging personal narratives, on the other hand, come from our own experiences, values, upbringing, and things that we genuinely believe to be true. It's important to know the difference.

———

Adjusting my 2013 TEDx talk to include my coming out story wasn't the only change that I made to the draft. I had planned to open my talk by performing "The Water Poem," which features earlier in this book. Originally the poem ended on an adversarial note, naming and shaming large multinational corporations involved in the exploitation of water resources around the world. When I wrote the poem, I had recently learned of the extent to which groundwater was being extracted and sold back to communities in poorer nations at exorbitant rates by large corporations, and I was appropriately outraged. As the event drew closer though, I realised I was uncomfortable with the confrontational nature of the ending. I had a gnawing feeling that these combative tactics might be doing more harm than good. Yelling, blaming, and finger pointing are easy to ignore. These companies are doing exactly what they were designed to do—increasing shareholder value —within an unjust and perverse economic system. The people who work for those corporations are probably good people who are just trying to provide for their families. Given that I knew this talk would exist on the internet in perpetuity, I took an alternative path and decided to rewrite the ending to the one that features in this book. I saw it as a softer landing, an invitation into philosophically considering a dark, unthinkable, and seriously water-short future in which human beings might be tapped to glean the water held within our bodies. It's the stuff of the worst dystopian nightmares, but in these times when reality is often stranger than fiction, it was a way to end on a thought-provoking note without blaming specific actors.

When I tested out my talk with a dear friend, I could see the pain on his face when he heard the new ending. He was a big fan of my original poem and someone who had a deep part of his identity rooted in activism and resistance against corporate interests. He told me that I had sold out—in slightly more polite words—and that I was censoring my art to be more palatable. In part, he was right; I *was* changing my message, and I was doing so intentionally to be more accessible to a wider audience. I didn't want to be speaking only to angry activists that were already primed to accept my message. Systems-level problems cannot be solved by only engaging with people that already think the way that we do, nor by directing vitriol towards those who think differently. The emergence of social media echo chambers display the fallacy of such tactics.

We likewise cannot tell people how to think: we can only invite them into a new story. As Audre Lorde said, we cannot undo the master's house with the same tools that were used to build it. If you're in the market of control, you can't control for good; there will always be an integrity missing. Rather than trying to force or trick people into believing in new narratives, it is more effective to act from our intrinsic values and expose the innate truth of our common humanity. While still feeling anger at the exploitation of people and the environment in the name of profit, I rewrote the ending of "The Water Poem" in an effort to meet people where they were at. For this particular audience, I felt that fighting fire with fire and using call-out tactics were not the most effective theories of change. That's not to say that there is never a time for protest or direct action—these tactics certainly have their place and have set monumental changes in motion. But I believe that these movements need to be accompanied by making space for reconciliation, for sharing our stories and experiences, and for letting our guard down long enough to understand each other. There are times to stand against something, and there are times to stand for something. I got great feedback about the poem when people spoke with me after my TEDx talk, and I didn't feel that changing the ending significantly changed the message.

Overcoming divisive thinking is not always easy work; after all, many of us are going up against a life time of us-vs-them conditioning and it's tempting to slip back into old habits. I ended up rewriting parts of this book towards the end of the process because some kind people who had read the draft pointed out that in some places I had inadvertently been doing exactly what I was telling my readers not to do, pointing fingers and othering people who thought differently. Failure to engage in an us-vs-them narrative does not mean denying the problems we face or giving in. Rather it means inviting people into different ways of thinking. I've come to realise that in many ways narrative work *is* activism. It's just a more subtle and nuanced kind of activism, and one that can underpin a kinder brand of politics, advocacy, media, and community engagement.

Developing platforms and opportunities to seek out and hear stories of those who are different from ourselves is an important step in this kind of activism. To overcome polarisation, we all have a responsibility to better understand one another and make space for sharing stories. A year after the terror attacks in Christchurch, a website called One Year On was launched sharing the stories of those in the Muslim community who had experienced the shootings first hand or lost loved ones. The stories paint a picture not only of survivors, widows, sons, daughters, and best friends, but also of people who loved to play soccer, ride bikes, climb mountains, and practise yoga. They are stories that feature both grief and humour, despair and hope, and they serve as glimpses into the multi-dimensional lives of the survivors. Around the same time, The Christchurch Invitation was developed by three members of the Christchurch Muslim community in discussion with others, to help overcome division and build communities that truly belong together. The Invitation, which is endorsed by the imams of the two mosques involved in the attacks, offers several simple core messages for anyone, based on a teaching of the Prophet Muhammad: spread peace, feed the hungry, and rebuild ties of kinship. The Invitation is grounded in the idea of reconnecting with others. A fourth part of the Prophet's original message is to pray at night while others are asleep—in a secular society like that of New Zealand, this has been construed as the simple invitation to reflect.

Tony Green is one member of that group from the Muslim community. Originally from the UK and a regular worshipper at Al Noor mosque for over twenty years, he acted as a media spokesperson for the mosque in the six months following the attacks. He explains the purpose behind The Christchurch Invitation:

In the wake of the terror attacks, we saw an outpouring of support from people around the world. We saw what it might look like when we viewed a person as a person and not through the distortions of a label. The Christchurch Invitation is just that; an invitation into connecting with people on a daily basis in four simple ways. It emphasises that we all have a role to play in overcoming division. The intention is not to proselytise—it is for people to look to their own values and to bring those values to the table. After the attacks, it felt like this community went 'from zero to hero' overnight; there was massive media attention, and we were wrenched from being off the radar into the global space of the wounded. What were we asking of this community, that they should be heroes for everyone else?

Tony points out that many in the Muslim community found it surprising that the world was so surprised by the response from the New Zealand public, prime minister, and the local community in Christchurch after the shootings:

> The degree to which New Zealand's response surprised the world said more about the world than it did about New Zealand. If empathy and unity in the wake of such a tragedy is surprising, what does that say about the state of human connection around the world?

At that time, when people asked him the question of how the community is doing, he would point out that "the community" is made up of people from forty-five or fifty different countries of origin; they come from a whole range of positions, experiences, and cultures. And just like any other group of people dealing with great grief, individuals were dealing with the tragedy in very different ways. The underlying assumption that "the Christchurch Muslim community" is one combined block of people who should all think and act the same is not a reasonable expectation of any group. The stories, values, experiences, and perspectives in any shared community of interest are diverse and multi-dimensional.

In that early period after the attacks, media would often ask Tony how "the community" was recovering and healing. It seemed odd to him to think that healing could be dictated by the calendar, or that healing could take place when the cause of the hurt had not been addressed. Tony would often reflect the question back to ask, "How have you changed?" Systemic social change begins with the small, daily actions of everyone. To me it appears that the real questions to ask are: "What is it that I can control? What can I do today to make change?"

The mother of one of the fifty-one victims of the Christchurch mosque shootings received her son's body on her birthday. In an extra cruel twist of fate, it was also Mother's Day in the Middle East, where she had grown up. She had as much reason as anyone to hate the man who took her son's life. Yet during his sentencing in court she looked the shooter straight in the eye and told him that she had chosen to forgive him and that she didn't hold any hate towards him. It was the only time that the attacker displayed any significant emotion during sentencing, giving her a slight nod, blinking heavily, and wiping his eye. On that day, this mother chose to embody a narrative of forgiveness and unity, rather than hate and division. She is not the only one. Others have forgiven too. Others have not, and that's completely understandable. But if even some of those who have suffered so much from the actions of somebody else's hate can forgive, then I believe there is much to be hopeful for.

13

WHOSE STORY IS THIS?

I was once at a Lean Startup conference where a young entrepreneur was hosting a session on "How to Build and Validate Your Startup in 45 Minutes." It was a gimmick of sorts, and he was aiming to demonstrate how quick and easy it could be to validate an idea, put together a simple landing page, and launch an offering of some kind. He encouraged audience participation and early on someone suggested that we collectively validate the business case for a hypothetical diet app to help people lose weight. Projecting his laptop onto a large screen behind him, the presenter worked in real time. He fired off a quick message on a consumer research platform, where ordinary people are paid small amounts of money to answer questions about anything that users care to ask about. Within a few minutes, someone had responded and suddenly the guy was on a call with a man somewhere in New York who was giving us intimate details of his struggles to lose weight. He sounded dejected, sharing how he had failed in so many different attempts. The room was silent and this person had no idea that his phone call was being broadcast live to a room of about 150 conference attendees. People started shifting uncomfortably in their seats, looking around at each other, and shuffling their notebooks. The obvious tension in the room only broke once the presenter hung up the phone call, and proceeded to fist pump the air and shout with excitement, receiving awkward applause. When I approached the presenter during the following tea break to bring to light his questionable ethics, he seemed amused and genuinely surprised that I had been offended. A few tweets featuring the event hashtag highlighted that I wasn't the only one who had been uncomfortable with someone unwittingly sharing a very personal story with a room full of strangers on the other side of the world.

Stories hold a great deal of power, and with that power comes the responsibility to use them carefully. Personal and cultural stories shared with others are a sacred gift, and should be treated as such. When tempted to share a story that isn't our own, we need to ask ourselves whether or not we have the right to tell it. We need to ask ourselves if we are the right person to tell that story, or if there is someone else who we don't typically hear from who might be better placed to tell it. Within our societies, some voices hold much more sway than others. We subconsciously weigh up the value and legitimacy of a story against the assumptions or beliefs we hold about the person telling it. We apply filters based on their social standing, background, race, position, perceived expertise, or personality, and we do it automatically in a microsecond. We tend to elevate the narratives and stories of those who have some degree of power or authority—politicians, celebrities, influencers, the media, thought leaders, and experts. Even the way we define those experts is itself formed by underlying narratives surrounding what sort of knowledge we value and who is qualified to use it. When we adopt the narratives of these powerful voices as truth, we leave many questions unasked and unanswered. Whose voices are missing? Whose stories are completely invisible to us? Whose narratives are edged out and silenced when certain groups or individuals take the limelight with their particular version of reality? Whose voice is the predominant narrative privileging, and how did they gain that privilege to speak louder in the first place?

Sometimes the answers are cultural. For example, in many conservative religious societies, women's voices are silenced. Women are still not allowed to be ordained as priests or ministers in some Christian denominations. In more progressive societies and communities, while there is more gender equality on the whole, the stories that still overwhelmingly underpin life are supported by a long history of social imbalances. Centuries of segregated gender roles, along with women's historical exclusion from voting, governing, and owning land (and hence the ability to create wealth from that land) have resulted in predominant narratives that are informed by the male worldview. Centuries of slavery and the conquering of nations by Anglo-Saxon and European powers have resulted in predominant narratives that are informed by the histories and power structures of those cultures. Centuries of discrimination against LGBTQ+ folks, aided by ongoing discrimination today, have resulted in narratives informed by heteronormativity. So when I say that many of our predominant Western narratives are informed by straight, white, cisgendered men, it is not intended as a criticism or attack on members of this particular subset of our society. It is purely stating a truth that the worldviews and versions of reality that are experienced by straight, white, cisgendered men have held a greatly disproportionate sway over our collective understanding of "the way things are." The thing is, the way things are is the product of inherent power dynamics that have been developed over many generations.

Identity politics receive a bad rap in some circles due to their focus on division and polarisation. But at the same time, they have facilitated so many conversations that are helping us to understand the systemic and intersectional natures of oppression. If these forces are left unacknowledged, the reality of whose voice get heard, who gets promoted, who gets acknowledged and cared for, and who gets paid fairly will always be skewed in favour of those who are privileged by the status quo. Unspoken narratives about power and privilege of voice have been upheld and exacerbated by the media, who for many are the gatekeepers of story. Particularly over the past few decades with the increased privatisation and merging of media outlets into powerful behemoths, there is a massive misalignment of ideals. Fair and balanced reporting has often been put aside to favour the perpetuation of stories that maximise profits and keep powerful people in power. A great deal of us from right across the political spectrum still do not question the sources of the media we consume and the motivations of the people running the organisations. We so easily forget to ask ourselves, *Whose story is this really?*

Among those who have suffered the most from the predominant narratives of white-centric, capitalist societies are Indigenous communities. The prevalent founding stories of many Western countries is still the one of the European colonising power arriving to create a "civilised society" and save Indigenous people from their "backwards ways." These narratives are still being taught to young children in schools. They inform our systems of food production, the ways we organise our households into nuclear families, our dominance over the natural world, and the ways in which we design our communities, towns, and cities. The mythical nature of many indigenous stories has been written off as non-scientific and superstitious. While a great number have been lost due to the systematic erasure of indigenous narratives, others have survived long enough to start gaining attention again in recent years. In this time when we are facing many interconnected ecological crises, we have much to learn from indigenous stories about how to live in harmony with the natural world. Once upon a time, long, long ago, we were all indigenous. We all inherently understood our connection to the living world around us. We were not masters over nature; we were nature— and we still are. But most of us have forgotten these ways of knowing, these myths that anchor us to the world that sustains us. Our elevation of rational, reductionist, and linear thought processes has severed us from our intuition and other subtle ways of knowing, and for those that have lived their whole life in big cities, the framing of ourselves as a part of nature may be completely foreign.

In some small but rapidly growing pockets of society, however, we are seeing a gravitation towards indigenous narratives of connection and the decolonisation of the stories that underpin our existence. I think we owe a great debt of gratitude to the keepers of those stories who have passed them along from one generation to another. A question I ask myself regularly is how can we be inspired by indigenous narratives to address the multi-dimensional pickles we find ourselves in? And, more importantly, how do we do so in such a way that avoids cultural appropriation or cherry-picking the parts that suit us without understanding the full nuance and subtleties that come along with them? Taking inspiration is one thing, but we need to be careful not to co-opt parts of a culture that is not ours. Sometimes we simply do not have the same words within our discourse to adequately understand indigenous concepts. For example, the Māori word kaitiakitanga is best translated as "guardianship" or "stewardship," and it is often used in reference to the land: that is, it is the act of serving as a protector. But in truth it is so much more nuanced than that, weaving in subtleties around relationships to place and duty of care to self and all people by looking after nature (because the two cannot be separated). We simply don't have a word in the English language that captures all of that. It's also important to remember that one Indigenous person's narrative might not be the same as another's. There are over one hundred Māori iwi and hapū (extended and smaller kinship groups, respectively) in New Zealand, and they each have different stories and narratives underpinning their culture.

The sharing of stories about marginalised people by those who have no lived experience of their situations can be a fate worse than erasure. Without any real sense of understanding and with unconscious bias often coming into play, the stories lack richness and context. Even when well intended, they may draw on or reinforce unhelpful tropes and stereotypes. In film and television the stories of individuals from minority groups follow common threads, often to support the storyline of a more mainstream protagonist. We see time and again the trope of the hilarious, camp, gay best friend in romantic comedies, who serves the sole purpose of being funny and supporting the heroine of the story. Also affecting queer narratives is the "Bury Your Gays" trope in film and TV shows where LGBTQ+ characters die at a much higher rate than heterosexual characters. This is especially true for women. A 2016 report[1] found a 31 percent death rate for queer women characters in television shows that aired between 1976 and 2016. Those who survived had a slim chance at a happy ending—the study reported a mere 10 percent of lesbian or bisexual women having positive closing arcs to their storyline.

Representation of marginalised groups in general is often missing. A 2021 study that analysed 200 top-grossing films released between 2017 and 2019 found that of the 8965 speaking characters identified, just 1.6% were Muslim.[2] In the real world, meanwhile, Muslims make up 24% of the global population. The study also found that 19% of Muslim primary and secondary characters died, more than half of them by violent means. Even more concerning, 39% of Muslim primary and secondary characters were the perpetrators of violence. Whether indirectly or directly, these types of stories reinforce the inaccurate narrative of Islam as a violent religion. The Black Best Friend, the Southern Hillbilly, or the Loud-Mouthed, Overbearing Latina are other examples of television tropes that emphasise a narrow, singular narrative of massively diverse groups of people. When we consume these singular stories, they risk becoming the defining narrative of that group and we don't see individuals for who they really are. The real story of one hilarious gay guy might be very different from the next hilarious gay guy. There are many different forms and interpretations of Islam. The story of one wheelchair user might be very different from another's. While representation and visibility of marginalised communities is improving, it is important to empower these voices to be able to tell their own stories. After all, we do not know what we do not know, and in telling the stories of others, our privilege and unconscious biases inevitably come into play.

Many efforts towards creating social and environmental change are launched with great intention, but with little meaningful input from the communities most affected or minimal effort to understand their guiding stories and narratives. We have romantic ideas of giving a voice to the voiceless, to shine a light on the stories that have gone untold or have been actively suppressed. But in our failure to truly understand the complexities, nuances, and needs of the communities we seek to help, we suffer from a sort of story-blindness and resort to filling the gaps with what we think we already know. This is not only an ineffective use of the time, money, and resources that are poured into campaigns and projects resulting in little tangible impact, it can also backfire and inflict more harm than good. If we are not truly listening to those who are most directly affected by a problem and actively involving them in developing solutions, then we risk perpetuating the same dominant narratives that have served to marginalise those people in the first place.

When the Canadian oil sands industry was looking to expand from Alberta into northern Saskatchewan in 2009, I worked on a campaign to put a pause on the exploration and development activities until more could be understood about the environmental effects. As part of my research and advocacy work, I was dispatched to a small town in the remote far north of the province, nestled into a tangle of rocks, wetlands, and untamed boreal forest. The town was at the epicentre of where the extraction activities were being proposed. I was there to connect with the locals, present at the school, understand the viewpoint of First Nations communities, and try to speak with as many community leaders as possible to present the environmental side of the debate. Despite my best efforts, I had been unable to set up many meetings prior to my departure. So I bumbled into town with half-baked plans and a list of names.

By modern Western standards, this town was struggling. Most of the streets weren't paved, the houses were modest at best and falling down in some instances, and there were stray dogs wandering the neighbourhood everywhere I went. I spent the first couple of days quizzing anyone who would chat with me, and managed to spend a few hours at the house of the town councillor who was the most vocally opposed to the proposed oil industry expansion. I sat at his kitchen table listening to his stories of being out on the land. He told ancestral tales of the old transport routes that his forebears had taken to trade furs and other goods. He spoke of how the pipelines would cut through these trails, in addition to disrupting the migration routes of caribou and other wildlife. The mayor of the town, on the other hand, hadn't been returning my phone calls. When I finally got through to her, she was at first cautiously interested in meeting with me and hearing me lay out the concerns of our organisation. She quickly changed her tune when she learned that I had spoken to the dissident councillor, and told me she was out of town all week so couldn't meet. Later that afternoon, I saw her driving her car down the main street of town.

After about three days of frustrating dead ends and feeling like my time in the north was slipping away, I took a drive out of town. I drove even further north with no particular purpose but to see the vast, sprawling boreal forest that was at risk of being destroyed. I had a moment of visceral connection with the wildness of the place when a lynx ran across the road in front of my car, trotted across the fire break, and paused to look back at me nonchalantly before disappearing once more amidst the spindly trees. Soaking in the pristine surroundings, I felt in utter despair. I was experiencing the feeling of being completely out of my depth, and unable to do anything about the situation. Faced with the enormity of the industry that I was up against, I was questioning what on Earth I was doing up there. Here was I trying to talk to a town full of people who were desperate for new economic livelihoods, and tell them that a new development was a bad thing. While some were concerned about the proposed oil sands activities, many of them had little precious mental energy to expend on something that was outside their immediate struggle of daily life. I pulled the car over and started doing what I do best. I wrote. I wrote of my frustrations. I wrote of the poverty and despair that I was witnessing. I wrote down many stream-of-consciousness thoughts that eventually became a poem. It was self-reflective in tone, outlining my confusion, discomfort, and feeling of helplessness at being able to enact any sort of meaningful change. The poem placed me at the centre of this particular story and focused almost exclusively on my experience of this place and my difficulties.

As I came to learn more about the nature of systemic inequalities and systems change, I eventually came to look back at my time in the north and the poem that I wrote, and realised that I had been going about it all wrong. I had sought some advice before heading north on best practice and protocols when engaging with First Nations and Métis communities and was going in with the best of intentions to actively listen and build relationships. However, I was operating subconsciously from the narrative and mentality of the *white saviour*. I had assumed that if I only went and talked to people, explaining the adverse environmental effects of oil sands development, that people would join the fight. I had assumed that if I highlighted the boom-bust nature of these sorts of projects that inevitably leave towns even worse off than before, that people would listen to me and understand. That they would somehow be grateful for the fact that I had driven for a day and a half to come and educate them. How wrong I was. And not only wrong, but as I have come to believe, actively destructive. By projecting my assumptions onto this community, I had been elevating my own and my organisation's narrative and theory of change above other voices and ways of knowing. I had been subconsciously undermining and devaluing their stories, their histories, and their versions of truth. I discounted their agency and ability to make decisions for themselves. That's not to say that the two narratives at play were incompatible. Indeed, there were many overlaps in the values that we both held and our mutual desires to see the great northern landscape preserved. But my narrative was incomplete and it was an outsider's one. Without realising it I had also been attempting to simplify a very complex situation that intersected across social, environmental, cultural, and economic lines. The community was desperate for any sort of economic stimulus, and it's true that some people would have gotten the much-needed jobs that the oil companies had promised (although history from Alberta pointed to the majority of the higher-paid skilled labour being brought in from outside the province).

Another important lesson I learned through this experience is that when you're a person with privilege, your good intentions can make it difficult for others to challenge you. When a person wants to help but is operating from a harmful narrative, for example that Western, colonised ways of thinking are always superior, it can place those who are detrimentally affected by that narrative in a tough spot. By challenging the harmful narrative or resulting actions, they risk casting themselves as argumentative or ungrateful for the offered help. It is hard for us to admit to ourselves that our good intentions are creating more harm than good, as we feel personally responsible. I think that while we are not directly responsible for the underlying narratives that inform our worldview, we do have a responsibility to question them when we find they are causing harm to others. Put simply, we are not responsible for the programming that we received from our upbringing, our privilege, the media, and other external messages, but we are responsible for installing the updates. Without doing so, we are perpetuating harmful assumptions and as such may inadvertently do damage. I had assumed that I knew what was best for this community. My poem even ended with the line "if I don't speak up, who will?" By uttering those seven words, I instantly discounted the voices of hundreds of people who were already speaking out against the proposed development. Voices of Indigenous leaders, voices of teachers, voices of local community advocates who were quietly organising in circles outside of my reach. Although I didn't think it consciously, I guess I had an underlying assumption that my voice carried more weight as a representative who had some of the province's best environmental scientists and policy strategists behind her. I was operating from a narrative instilled upon me by a process and culture of colonisation. I was certainly naive in thinking that I would be able to gain the trust of the people I was speaking to within a week. My second trip up there was marginally more successful in terms of relationship building, but was nonetheless still tough going. The people in the north had seen people like me coming and going for years, and I now understand the distrust with which they regarded me.

I haven't performed that poem for many years now, as the white saviour story is not one I'm willing to align myself with any more. That's not to say that I won't slip up and fall into old patterns, as I have a lifetime of social conditioning to grapple with. But it's a story that I am trying my best to constantly question and check myself against. In many places, the hero narratives of Western colonisation are unravelling as we realise how laced they are with exploitation, the forceful change of culture, and the erasure of indigenous stories. Elevating and making space for the stories that have historically gone untold requires coming in with a genuine willingness to listen without recourse, to be called out, to sit with discomfort, and to meet people where they are at. It's a journey of humility steeped in a willingness to unlearn much of what we have been taught, both explicitly and implicitly. It means giving voice to those whose voices have been silenced for so long. For that to happen we need to practise the art of story-listening alongside that of storytelling. After all, every act of storytelling is based in a collaborative relationship between two parties—the teller of the story, and the receiver. Without nurturing both skill sets, the richness, meaning, and lessons embedded in our stories risk being lost to the ether, never to land.

14

THE SUBTLE ART OF STORY-LISTENING

In the early days of writing this book, I was hiking with my father and sister in one of New Zealand's incredible regions of native bush, Te Urewera. This particular region was unique in that it had formerly been a national park, which in 2014 was returned to the mana whenua Tūhoe—the original Māori custodians, or kaitiaki, of that land. Not only was it returned to Tūhoe to protect and hold governance over, but it also gained legal personhood status. It was the first specific piece of land in the world to have achieved such a position, following the lead of Ecuador and Bolivia who had granted rights to nature more generally. The move represented a significant shift in narrative from nature as an abstract thing to a living thing with rights. A rainforest shrouded in mist, Te Urewera is a truly special place with an ancient energy to it, of great significance to the Tūhoe iwi. We were staying in a backcountry hut managed by the Department of Conservation (DOC), one of almost a thousand spread throughout the country that are available to hikers, hunters, tourists, and other visitors alike, for a small nightly fee. Sharing our accommodation was a local man named Ron.

A retired farmer and a life-long hunter, Ron hated DOC with a vengeance. He was staunchly against the use of 1080 poison (sodium fluoroacetate), which is used across New Zealand to manage introduced predator species such as possums, rats, and stoats. The use of 1080 is highly controversial in New Zealand, with critics opposing it on the grounds that it results in a slow and painful death and the fact that it can also kill non-target species including native birds, deer, dogs, insects, reptiles, and fish. Supporters contend that, while not perfect, 1080 is the only practical, fast, and cost-effective means of removing the predators that prey upon New Zealand's native bird species, 80 percent of which are endangered or in some form of trouble.[1] Without predator control, nine out of ten Kiwi chicks, New Zealand's iconic native bird, are killed within the first twelve months of life. Many other native bird species have already been predated into extinction. As a former DOC employee involved in conservation and predator control, I found myself reacting strongly to some of Ron's claims that the pests don't actually do much harm. I considered his comments to be bordering on ludicrous and completely at odds with what the science was telling us. Despite my scepticism, I chose to listen with curiosity and empathy. I can appreciate both sides of the 1080 argument, and the inherent complexity involved means I am not committed to a firm position either way. Yet my historical association with DOC saw my subconscious walls going up. I didn't mention to Ron that I was a former employee of his loathed foe, but even as he asked me with a sidelong glance what I thought of our current prime minister, I could see he was sizing me up to decide whether I was with him or against him.

As he spoke, it became clear to me that he was coming from a place not just of passion and anger, but more tellingly a place of grief for what he had lost over the past forty years of hunting and farming. He had watched the decline of many of our native birds over the years, and had witnessed hunting dogs who had consumed 1080 writhing in their final death throes. He had seen livelihoods affected as families who relied on hunting deer for a source of sustenance experienced declining populations after aerial drops of the poison. After a while, we shifted the conversation to regenerative agriculture and there we found some common ground. He told me of the work he had done on his kiwifruit orchard, in which he used only biodynamic methods of farming. Within three years of conversion after taking over the orchard, he had been out-producing his commercial neighbours who used conventional fruit-growing methods, and boasted one of the lowest fruit rejection rates by sorting and packing sheds in the region. In turn, I relayed stories of some of the farmers, scientists, and advocates I had been talking to recently, as part of my research to produce a series of articles on the regenerative agriculture opportunity for New Zealand. As Ron felt my open response and active, empathetic listening to his story, and heard stories from me that derived from a similar set of values, he visibly softened. He looked me in the eye more frequently, dropped his shoulders, and spoke with less of an edge in his voice. From there on in, he seemed more open to the things I had to say on all topics. By identifying common threads in our stories, we nurtured a mutual safe zone where our voice spoke to more receptive ears.

When we are sharing stories in person, we assume that the person telling the story is the one who is in control, but the listener or receiver of that story also holds great power. It is a real skill and a gift to listen authentically, resisting the urge to formulate a response in your head triggered by things that the other person is saying. So often when someone is telling a story, we are filtering the words through a set of assumptions, values, and preconceived notions of who this person is, their social standing, authority, or supposed legitimacy to tell that story. We are reading between the lines, looking for clues as to whether someone broadly agrees with us or not, or whether we consider their point of view of interest to us. The antidote to this often subconscious behaviour is deep and authentic story-listening.

When we really and truly listen to someone's story, we ignore all those filters and lenses and relegate ourselves to a place of beginner's mind. Assuming nothing, we elevate the storyteller to the role of expert, viewing them as the ultimate authority on their own life and truth. When we sit with the discomfort of silence, threads of story emerge that wouldn't see the light of day in rushed conversation. When we listen intently without judgment or praise, we open the way to more than just an intellectual understanding of another person's point of view. We gain a much deeper awareness of the human emotions, values, and series of experiences that led to that view. Receiving someone's story without applying any of your subconscious filters allows stories to exist in their pure form, messy and incomplete. They aren't good, they aren't bad—they just are. We aren't looking for a preconceived answer or foregone conclusion, no matter how similar the story might sound to another one we've heard before. Nor are we looking for a lesson or the enlightening aha moment that will draw everything together. Story-listening helps us to value collective knowledge, and to understand much more than we could possibly know from our own experiences alone. It is the same model of deep listening that we see in collective group processes such as those promoted by Alcoholics Anonymous and other twelve-step programmes, Bible study groups, carefully facilitated retreats, women's and men's circles, and other communities that provide space for dialogue, reflection, and the sharing of experience. But most of us no longer have regular opportunities to sit around in circles facing each other in all our human glory and imperfection. With so many of our social interactions taking place online, we may instead find ourselves shouting past each other until we are red in the face at the audacity, the gall, the supposed stupidity of *"those other people."*

For deep and genuine story-listening to occur, certain rituals, rules, guidelines, or expected group or community behaviours and norms can help to create a safe, sacred space between the storyteller and the story-listener and support the emergence of rich storytelling. The culture of the group needs to define whether or not it is appropriate to ask questions or actively participate beyond listening. Audience participation, for example, is a significant part of the spoken word poetry scene, especially during the competitive slams. In fact, in most poetry slams, the judges in the audience are instructed by the MC to score poets partly based on audience reaction, in addition to content and delivery. Inspired by the beatnik poets of the 50s and 60s, audience members often snap their fingers when they are moved or when they agree with something that the poet is saying. These little rituals help to build the cohesive threads of community, and show the poet that the audience is really listening. For myself, it also had the tandem effect of helping me to actually engage with what the poet on stage was saying, rather than nervously thinking about my own upcoming turn on the stage and running through the lines of my poem in my head.

In part, I think our collective lack of ability to truly listen is both a symptom and cause of today's polarised world and the state of public discourse. We are so used to just waiting for our turn to talk and refute the other person's point of view that we don't hear what they're saying. I also think it is symptomatic of the perceived scarcity of time that we each have in today's busy world. Our lives are filled with commitments, deadlines, responsibilities, after-school activities for the kids, working one or more jobs, and transporting ourselves and our families around. The work of actively listening and seeking to understand others is one that takes time and commitment, and the nature of our modern lives and organisations are underpinned by a narrative of time scarcity. At work, the day-to-day rush of finishing that meeting on time, delivering that campaign, or shipping that product leaves very little space to truly listen and hear what our colleagues or other stakeholders have to say. But by rushing through, we miss out on the richness and context that could be gained with more time to listen, and we risk talking past each other. I think this is part of the reason so many seemingly well-intended projects or campaigns fail to achieve the impact that they set out to create; they didn't allow for enough deep listening time to properly diagnose all angles of a problem. This is further complicated and nuanced by the fact that we are biased in terms of whose stories or narratives hold more value, and we tend to forget that the hierarchical structures that inform these biases are built upon historical power imbalances.

At one of the impact leader summits that the Edmund Hillary Fellowship (EHF) hosted regularly, one of the EHF fellows was facilitating a session on a proposed environmental policy framework that a group of fellows were investigating for New Zealand. She was seeking feedback from summit participants about the framework, and had attracted about fifty people to the session. Shortly after starting, she mentioned that her organisation had engaged with the local Māori iwi , along with other iwi/Māori, to get their input, seek their views, and test whether they saw value in exploring the framework. A respected Māori elder from the iwi happened to be present in the circle, and she interjected stating that she did not feel that they had been adequately engaged. She offered that while the framework had merit, her iwi still had some serious reservations that needed to be addressed. The EHF fellow responded, trying to smooth over the interjection and continue with the session, but the elder was firm in her criticisms of the consultation process and pressed the fellow. Over the course of the following hour or so, what transpired was a glimpse into the complexities of understanding one another when two parties are coming from very different worldviews, with different narratives, belief systems, and cultural norms. Within Māori culture, the process of consultation, discussion, and decision-making is one that is seldom time-bound. There are variations in the ways that such a process is conducted, depending on the tikanga or cultural practices of a particular iwi or hapū, but by and large it is a process that is only complete when anyone who wants to have a say has finished talking. Traditionally, it is a process that may go on for days or even weeks, and it cannot be rushed. Additionally, the Māori view of humankind's relationship with the natural environment is worlds apart from the approach that typifies environmental policy development in most Western nations. As with most indigenous cultures, there is no separation between people and nature. People *are* part of the natural world. People *are* nature. Within this worldview, people anchor their ancestry and identity to a specific mountain and river or other body of water. So the elder was not just speaking for herself and her people, but also on behalf of many ancestors, her ancestral land, and the countless generations yet to be born. Coming up against the idea of adopting a framework in New Zealand that had been developed overseas, and against the defined process of policy development with its timelines, myriad accountabilities, vastly different decision-making processes, and notions of "governance" over the natural environment, there was much scope for miscommunication and misunderstanding. The situation wasn't unique but rather represents a lack of genuine understanding of indigenous worldviews that is systemic across many organisations everywhere.

At the time of its formation, EHF had established a partnership with the local iwi, in effect agreeing that the two parties would support and stand by each other in the spirit of reciprocity and mutual trust. From this foundation, and given that it was an EHF-hosted event, the session ceased to be a discussion led by the EHF fellow about the project, and instead emerged into an open sharing session. We talked about the ways in which different people and groups talk past each other, and the historical and ongoing harms that government policy, processes, and actions have inflicted upon Māori in New Zealand. The situation also exposed different interpretations and misunderstandings about the nature of the relationship between EHF and the local iwi, what it meant, and what our responsibilities were to support one another. As an EHF staff member and a Pākehā (a New Zealander of European descent), it was deeply uncomfortable at times, drawing on histories of the New Zealand Wars and land confiscations, broken promises, and a lack of adherence by the Crown to te Tiriti o Waitangi (the Treaty of Waitangi), the founding document of New Zealand. But ultimately, it was an exercise in demonstrating the need for patient and authentic listening, and was an incredible learning experience for those present. Of course, the short time provided for the session meant it barely touched upon the vast complexities at play, but it highlighted for me how much work we have yet to do to really understand each other's stories and narratives. It served as a glimpse into how we might better build knowledge together, and create frameworks that will work for all the people of New Zealand. The application of indigenous wisdom, knowledge, and worldviews into policy-making is a lofty goal, and I would argue a necessary one if we are to avoid total ecological collapse in the coming decades. But trust levels are understandably low, and it will be very difficult to do unless everyone is willing to genuinely listen and seek to understand one another. Anything else risks perpetuating the same lip service that we have seen for so long.

The examples above largely focus on the art of story-listening with the intent to simply hear and understand a person's point of view, not to change it. But when we are trying to find solutions to systemic problems, we are often seeking to bring people along with us. Perhaps we are trying to nurture more tolerant views, cultivate a deeper sense of connection, or allay fears about a real or imagined other. Our tactics may be quite different if we are listening to someone with the intent of hoping to change their views. Many of the same practices of genuine, non-judgmental listening apply, but with the addition of a considered right of reply that seeks to unpack their fears. We may offer a counter-story that provides an alternative perspective, or ask inviting questions that help us to better understand, while creating opportunities to gently probe and challenge predominant narratives, misconceptions, or stereotypes.

Recent research supports the idea that sharing stories can change a person's deeply held point of view on divisive topics, in ways that the exchange of rational argument cannot. A wide-reaching study, published in *American Political Science Review*, investigated whether it was possible to change exclusionary attitudes towards undocumented immigrants and transgender people. In three field experiments, 230 canvassers conversed with 6869 voters across seven US locations, engaging them either over the phone or face-to-face by knocking on doors.[2] They found that while conversations deploying arguments alone had no effects on voters' exclusionary immigration policy or discriminatory attitudes, otherwise identical conversations that also included the non-judgmental exchange of stories significantly reduced exclusionary attitudes for at least four months following the conversation. By first listening carefully without judgment to the concerns of the voters whose doors they knocked on, canvassers then shared stories of transgender individuals or undocumented immigrants that they knew, in the sort of conversational tone you might expect from a couple of friends chatting over a beer down at the pub or café. No arguing, no defensiveness, just telling stories and sharing how current exclusionary policies affect the lives of real people. Imagine if all our major policy decisions were made in such a welcoming, inclusive, and non-judgmental way.

After any kind of deep story-listening work, the narratives of both parties may emerge with a new richness of understanding. The act of listening from neutral ground legitimises the story in the other person, helps them to drop their armour, and to be more open. Like any new or unfamiliar practice though (and I would argue that it's unfamiliar to a great many of us), the act of story-listening is a muscle that needs to be flexed often. In group situations of more than three or four people, the practice works best with the golden trifecta of a skilled facilitator, a genuine willingness from all participants to listen, and enough dedicated time to ensure that everyone can be fully heard. With any number of participants, it requires a conscious decision not to fall into old patterns and jump to conclusions. It requires developing spaces and practices for people to feel safe enough to authentically share without fear of reprisal or judgment.

15

STRANGE BEDFELLOWS

It was at a youth climate change summit in 2012 that Xena Warrior Princess told me that the best way to enact long-lasting structural change was to get into bed with strange bedfellows. Laced in metaphor, it was a suggestion to break outside our own bubbles and work with people who think differently from ourselves. In truth, it was a message delivered not by Xena herself but by Lucy Lawless, the actress who had played Xena in the 90s fantasy TV series (but that's not nearly as good a story). Previously I understood the need to seek out collaborators who thought differently from me, people I wouldn't usually look to work with. But the framing of those people as someone who I might share a bed with was an interesting one. It led me to wonder if the same level of depth, familiarity, trust, and intimacy is needed between diverse players looking to achieve systems change together, as those who might fall into bed together. Of course, people who have very little familiarity with each other sometimes find themselves in bed together, but that's not necessarily the best recipe for a solid long-term relationship. With the converging crises and systemic challenges that the world is facing, we need coordinated responses involving many different people in order to develop cohesive narratives of the future and avoid siloed efforts.

The cohort structure underpinning the Edmund Hillary Fellowship (EHF) was designed exactly for this purpose. The selection process brought together people who were working in vastly different ways towards myriad problems, but were united by a shared set of values and a vision for a better future. The week-long induction retreats saw space industry experts sitting at the dinner table next to people who were working at the grassroots level to drive social change. Silicon Valley venture capitalists were talking with regenerative farmers who were advocating for a drastic change in mindset in the way that we grow food. Businesswomen from Palestine and Azerbaijan were connecting with some of the world's leading experts on blockchains and peer-to-peer technologies. Ideas shared over a meal became tangible cross-disciplinary projects within a matter of weeks, and relationships were forged that could last well beyond individual ventures. By bringing together people with diverse viewpoints and theories of change who shared a desire to shift business-as-usual narratives, it was our team's hope that we could provide the fertile soil from which the seeds of systems change could sprout. Cohort sizes ranged from thirty to one hundred individuals, getting progressively larger as the programme developed, and we reserved roughly 20 percent of the spaces for New Zealanders. They didn't need the Global Impact Visa, of course, but by joining the fellowship they were able to help international fellows to integrate and quickly form relationships within New Zealand's business, government, and entrepreneurial ecosystem. In turn, the international fellows opened their networks to Kiwi entrepreneurs and change agents, connecting them with investors, industry experts, and potential collaborators across the world. Many of the fellows had worked at a multinational level across a number of industries, and brought with them specialist knowledge of the complexities of the problems they were tackling. The chance to bump up against people who were outside their usual circles helped to deepen everyone's understanding of the systemic nature of global problems and the need for cross-sector, cross-industry cooperation.

While many other fellowship programmes tend to favour a specific age demographic, there is almost a half century's age range within EHF with fellows ranging from twenty-one to seventy. We made a point of accepting fellows of all ages, in recognition that intergenerational knowledge transfer is crucial to understanding complex problems and developing nuanced solutions. Within many Western cultures, there is a lot of value placed on youth and newness in general. This is exacerbated by our faith in shiny new technologies to solve our problems and a global advertising industry that feeds on our fears and insecurities. But we have so much to learn from our elders when it comes to understanding human nature, cyclical patterns, and the effects of historical social and political events that happened before some of us were even born. The eldest EHF fellow is a well-respected Kiwi business journalist who worked for the *Financial Times* in London and New York between 1979 and 1997, covering the height of Thatcherism and three major financial crashes, in 1987, 1997, and 2007/08. He is now a big proponent for systems thinking, impact-based business, and regenerative economies, and brings invaluable knowledge and perspective to the young and keen entrepreneurs, particularly those working in financial technologies. Equally, the ideas and dreams of the young in our society are often dismissed by those who consider themselves older and wiser. Governance boards around the world are dominated by those who are these days sporting grey hairs, the vast majority of them men. But without representation from the younger generation, they risk being wildly out of touch with a rapidly changing world. The youngest EHF fellow produces purpose-driven film and media and is keenly involved in the regenerative agriculture movement. Bringing an understanding of the latest trends in visual storytelling to inspire change is of huge value to the more analytical entrepreneurs and traditional investors in the community, who are more used to crunching numbers than thinking about how stories can move people.

The coming together of passionate people through EHF resulted in some wonderful collaborations. A conversation between a Māori rights advocate and some blockchain entrepreneurs at the first cohort's induction week was the beginning of a new venture that aims to provide Māori iwi and communities with a platform to own, access, and manage sovereignty over their data using blockchain technology. A lawyer and healthcare activist teamed up with a health strategist in New York to work on an initiative to make the Pacific Island nation of Niue the first country in the world to be free of hepatitis B and C. Another project saw a young Palestinian entrepreneur and a British fellow working in suicide prevention and youth empowerment in the tea estates of Sri Lanka. They additionally worked with a young Māori change-maker to host a series of learning conversations where refugee youth in Auckland could share migration stories, narratives that were important to them, and bring their whole selves into the room. The more I witnessed these strange and glorious collaborations coming out of the programme, the more I was able to believe in humanity's ability to solve complex, global challenges in healthcare, education, climate, social inequality, human rights, indigenous rights, technology, the economy, the future of food, and everything in between. I was beginning to see how important it was to invite strange bedfellows into the fold to collectively rewrite the narratives of the future.

That's not to say that it will be easy. It takes a lot of dedicated work to bring together different factions of government, charities, community organisations, and businesses to coalesce around a central narrative, with each attached to their own diverse theories of change. One framework that I think holds great promise for transformative narrative change is that of Collective Impact. First highlighted in an article in *Stanford Social Innovation Review* in 2011, this framework sets out a specific process through which diverse actors from different sectors can agree to a shared vision for solving a specific social or environmental problem. While collaboration is nothing new, the Collective Impact model goes several steps further to embed a carefully structured process, shared systems of measurement, a culture of continuous communication, mutually reinforcing activities, and a centralised backbone organisation with dedicated staff. One EHF fellow, Janette Searle, has seen great results from facilitating a Collective Impact process designed to improve mental health, wellbeing, and education outcomes for youth in West Auckland. The area faced a number of challenges with young people, including drug use, violence, and a high rate of expulsion from schools. The Achieving at Waitakere Collective Impact Initiative pulled together a wide range of stakeholders in the community. The group included the principals of twelve high schools and several other primary and middle schools, the local district health board, local cultural groups, youth action organisations, local business associations, several philanthropic foundations, a large grocery store chain, Auckland Council, the New Zealand Police, and government ministers and senior leadership from both the Ministry of Education and Oranga

Tamariki, New Zealand's Ministry for Children. In line with Collective Impact best practice, the group encouraged the leaders of organisations to join the initiative rather than have them send more junior personnel. This helped create high-level buy-in.

One of the programmes that the initiative ran was focused on youth who were at risk of being excluded from school due to challenging behaviours, many of whom were already in alternative education. The goal was to keep them engaged in education, and for those that were capable, transition them back into the mainstream school system, have them getting on with their teachers and peers, and achieving good educational outcomes. In 2016 before the programme began, just 10 percent of thirteen- to sixteen-year-olds who left alternative education went on to further education, training, or employment. The following year, after the programme was introduced, that figure jumped to 51 percent and in 2018, when the programme was moved under government contract, it increased further to 74 percent.

The numbers are impressive, but Janette also tells a compelling story of a young man who had been kicked out of mainstream education early in his schooling days. He was head of a youth gang, involved in drugs and violence, and had been through the justice system and multiple homes. After getting involved with Achieving at Waitakere's programmes, he became one of their biggest success stories. He graduated from a local institute of technology with a carpentry qualification, became fully employed, and hasn't had any run-ins with the criminal justice system since he got involved. Janette notes he's had a positive knock-on effect on his siblings and improved outcomes in his family life. The young man recently told her that if he hadn't been involved in the programme, he is sure he would have been either in jail or dead by now. The Achieving at Waitakere initiative started out with a vision and high-level narrative of what the future of education could look like for young people in the area. Janette credits the success of the initiative with the willingness of stakeholders to believe in this shared narrative. They also showed a willingness to reframe themselves from being service providers limited by bureaucracy to active problem-solvers who would frequently ask the question, *What is best for the young person?* While before young people were bounced between different organisations because a particular problem or situation didn't fit exactly within certain mandates, this reframe allowed stakeholders to bend the boundaries of organisational responsibility and place the young person at the centre of their narrative of change. For those who want to truly shift systems, we need to ask ourselves whether we are brave enough to challenge the long-held assumptions that we have, admit that our approaches might have been wrong or ineffective in the past, and be willing to work with others who think differently towards better outcomes.

New York-based Narrative Initiative is an organisation that is a global leader in bringing together diverse actors towards narrative change. Founded in early 2017 with significant funding from the Atlantic Philanthropies and Ford Foundation, the Narrative Initiative connects an international network of narrative specialists, amplifies emerging tools and methodologies, and activates new collaborations that lead to greater alignment on narratives of social change. Stumbling upon their seminal 2017 report "Toward New Gravity" was a game-changer for me in terms of understanding the different elements of narrative change.[1] Capturing learnings from interviews with over one hundred thought leaders in cognitive and social sciences, strategic communications, movement building, storytelling, big data, and the arts, the report provided a timely snapshot of the state of the narrative change landscape. It also served as a rallying cry to bring people together, as described by their founding former CEO, Jee Kim:

> I think there's a new level of cohesion amongst disparate actors and thinkers that didn't exist a few years ago. Beacons that have been put out in the world like Toward New Gravity and other efforts called people to realise, okay, I'm part of a tribe.

In order to achieve lasting social change, Jee describes a cycle of four key stages: analysis of dominant societal narratives; defining and creating the narratives that you wish to see gain traction; disseminating those narratives; and then observing how they are performing and reiterating as necessary.

Within that cycle, Jee believes that there is a common blindspot in many well-intended efforts. He sees a great deal of energy being put into the analysis of the narratives that are doing us harm and the creation of new ones but believes there isn't sufficient attention being paid to leveraging the best dissemination channels to get the message out there, both online and in-person. Pop culture is one place where people who seek to make change don't usually look, but that's exactly where it may be most effective to focus efforts. Jee says:

> We have certainly seen some success in the last two decades with social issue documentaries and concentrated efforts on influencing Hollywood, but at the same time quick-fire content platforms like TikTok have emerged and young people's attention is simply not focused on the older twentieth century modes of distribution. I'm concerned that we're not always thinking quite as hard and rigorously as we should about the

question of dissemination. Transmitting new narratives is also about human associations and networks—religious institutions, trade unions, block associations, cultural associations, parent-teacher associations—these can be massive, powerful disseminators of new narratives if we to tap into them.

He also believes that we need a wide-scale return to simplicity, and for those who are interested in shifting narratives to walk the talk when it comes to crafting a compelling story:

> I've seen way too many movements, initiatives, or campaigns get bogged down, especially when it's coalitional, because people trip over individual words when the point is not the individual words, but rather how compelling the aggregate of the narrative is as their vehicle. I'm speculating, but think partly it's thanks to the muscle memory of advocates and rights lawyers who have too much specialised education and are obsessed with footnoting things, instead of developing emotionally resonant, concise narratives along with storylines, brands, and images that can capture the imagination.

This is where the true power of the UN's Sustainable Development Goals (SDGs) lie. At their core, they are a set of seventeen simple statements that paint a narrative of a global future that is very different from today. The goals have been criticised for being difficult to implement, quantify, and monitor. But it is precisely their simplicity that makes them so powerful as narratives; they provide a high-level story that we can all orient our efforts towards. They paint a vision of a better world—a world in which there is less suffering, more joy, a healthier biosphere, and a global population that is more at peace with each other and the planet we call home. How they are implemented at a national and regional level is highly contextual, but we also need to find ways to make them work together. Of the seventeen goals, I believe the last one, "Partnerships for the Goals," is by far the most important. In my view, it should have been listed as number one to underscore the gravity of the need to work together towards solving the other sixteen in an integrated way. For the SDGs to have a chance at delivering on their lofty promises, we need to work towards them in a systemic way that recognises the interconnected nature of the problems they address. To realise their promise, each of the new narratives that the SDGs describe needs to shift together. No one goal is more important than the others because they are all interconnected. It's not a case of *either/or*, but rather needs to be many layers of *and*. The UN is doing some good work in assessing the interactions and synergies between different goals, particularly as they relate to climate change.

To truly enact change at the pace we need, however, we need millions of diverse efforts around the world simultaneously working in an integrated and collective way. We need to invite diverse groups of people to the table, in ways that empower and inspire. The work that we have ahead of us will be a lonely road if we don't have others by our side. After all, we are going up against nothing less than the powerful, deeply ingrained stories and myths that have come to dictate our lives, behaviours, cultures, and attitudes. Everywhere we turn, the old extractive and divisive narratives are lurking, trying to course correct us back to "the way things are." The great challenge of working at scale in an integrated way is of course the fact that it is impossible to communicate with everyone. Even if we had back-to-back video calls every day for the rest of our working lives, it would be impossible to keep tabs on all the other aligned efforts that are working towards similar goals. As Yuval Noah Harari highlighted in his influential book *Sapiens*, the key cognitive shift in early humans that allowed us to begin cooperating in much larger groups some seventy thousand years ago was our ability to tell and believe in stories and myths.[2] To shift from a primitive species that communicated in grunts and gestures, we needed to have some sort of shared understanding of reality that wraps truth up in story, to guide us into the future. And now, in this post-truth world we find ourselves in, we need this again more than ever before.

The disruptions brought about by the COVID-19 pandemic have presented us with the opportunity to closely examine many of the narratives that underpin our lives, and to understand how they enable the status quo and hinder change. I believe that the key to riding this momentum and shifting the predominant narratives of our time lies in collective adherence to central guiding myths that large communities of diverse humans can believe in. Myths that don't explain the how, but the why. Narratives that shine a light on the path, revealing where it is heading. Stories that serve as a compass, rather than a map. In the final section of this book, I briefly outline ten new myths for humanity along with corresponding stories, frames, and narratives that can guide our species towards becoming a version of ourselves that is wiser, kinder, more regenerative, and lives in harmony with the rest of the world.

TEN NEW MYTHS FOR HUMANITY

THE ONE THAT HASN'T BEEN WRITTEN YET

Watch a video of this poem

Once upon a time,
when limestone was the roof above our head and faces
    danced in firelight,
we looked to the stars in jealousy,
the home fires of the gods.

Once upon a time,
when myth was the carrier of culture,
and Earth was host to the home fire burning between
    mother and child,
the rivers flowed within our veins,

of nourishment, unconditional,
bloodline connections, unequivocal,
the ever-present reminder of something larger than self.

Then fire became steam
and steam drove fire through the wires
to bring us everything we desired,
and here we find ourselves today.

In the months following my move away to university,
my mother would send me a recurring text message.
The same three little words every time.
She would write,
ET, phone home.

A fledgling spreading wings,
flight from the nest a necessity,
yet I felt the guilt at the frequency
by which those three little words arrived.
To this day, I am ashamed by how often
the message still applies.

Just a cellular signal away, yet we are worlds apart.

We evolved as tribal creatures,
never meant to live this way.
Yet our modern tribes are insular, singular thinking,
a narrow subset of the village.

For every fibre optic cable that is laid beneath our feet,
an invisible wall arises.
For every progression towards a faster connection,
we step further away from the analogue of face-to-face
     interaction.

But life doesn't happen in front of screens—
that world is merely a facsimile of that which is right
    before us,
if we would only choose to look.

We speak of depression and anxiety as mental illness
yet really they are ailments of the heart—
symptoms of a sick society.

A metaphorical galaxy, our degree of disconnection.

We have taken to holding our own hands beneath the
    pillow
so no one can see how lonely we have become.
Our day-to-day transactions so impersonal
that we feel the need to print faces on our money
to maintain some semblance of a human touch.

The future though,
the one that hasn't been written yet,
the only we hardly dare imagine,
holds its hopeful promise in looking to the past.
It's not too late to take a different path,
our bridges not so much burned, as forgotten.

Trim back the overgrowth along those abandoned
    country lanes,
and we will find that it is we ourselves who are the
    cobblestones
that make up the path to connection.

It's we, who are the bloodlines.
It's we, who are the phone wires.
It's we, who hold the keys to that intangible something

that we know, deep down,
is missing from our lives.

ET, call your mother.
Warm your bones at the home fires of your ancestors.
There's a chance we can still remember where we came
     from,
back when the analogue was fire.

———

*To view the video of this poem, follow the link below or scan the QR
code at the beginning of the poem.*

alinasiegfried.com/not-written-yet

16

____

FROM ME TO WE

Current narrative: *It's everyone for themselves, and we are each responsible for our own circumstances.*
New myth: *The fate of each human on Earth is inextricably intertwined with the fate of everyone else.*

WHENEVER I FEEL DOWN ABOUT THE DEGREE TO WHICH PEOPLE are disconnected from each other in our fast-paced, modern lives, I watch videos of flash mobs on the internet. There is something magical about watching dozens of people in a busy place seemingly going about their everyday individual lives suddenly disrupting the illusion of separation and coming together as one cohesive, cooperative unit. The looks of pure delight from bystanders who happened to be in the right place at the right time has an essence of unadulterated joy that we seldom see on the faces of strangers. Our movement through public spaces is so often a solitary experience, as we make our way through the train station with headphones blocking out everyone else, that when we witness a collective experience that wasn't expected it is something truly special and unusual.

Since Thatcherism in the UK, Reaganomics in the US, Rogernomics in New Zealand, Australia's economic rationalism, and other neoliberal shifts of the 1980s, there has been a broad-scale move in many Western nations towards a deep-seated narrative of individualism. Thatcher famously went as far as to say, "There is no such thing as society. There are individuals, and there are families." This sentiment has struck a particular chord in the United States, where the narrative of the American Dream still drives culture and politics, despite it being increasingly more farcical by the year. The American Dream tells the pervasive story that anyone can achieve their own version of success, be upwardly mobile, and improve their lot in life, regardless of who they are, provided that they sacrifice enough, work hard enough, and are prepared to take a few risks along the way. America might be the poster child for the rags-to-riches story, but many other Western cultures experience a watered-down version of the same narrative, which has deep roots within the colonial ideals of freedom, opportunity, and capitalism. It is the story that underpins the global self-help and personal development industry, the value of which is forecast to reach US$56.7 billion dollars by 2027.[1] And it utterly fails to recognise that we don't, in fact, live in a vacuum.

The narrative of individualism suggests that we don't *need* other people. Nothing could be further from the truth. Human beings are social creatures, we evolved to work together. While self-help teachings can be hugely beneficial, they often distract us from the fact that many of our successes and failures are influenced by factors completely outside our control. Those who consider themselves self-made have other people intricately tied up in their successes, many of them unrecognised or under-appreciated. Similarly, those who are homeless, living in poverty, suffering from ill health, or who are otherwise struggling, are under constant pressure from a system that tells them that they are wholly responsible for their own situations, regardless of external factors. The narrative of personal responsibility has played a significant role in the evolution of deeply individualistic societies in which loneliness, depression, anxiety, and othering are rife.

When I say "we," who is it that comes to mind? Is it you and me? Is it all of the people who are reading this book? Is it your tribe, perhaps, your church congregation, your community, your family, or group of friends? Of course, "we" is contextual, so maybe you're thinking, *It depends ...* What if "we" was everyone on Earth? We humans, us *Homo sapiens*. Our ability to cooperate in small-to-medium-sized groups of others has played a huge role in humanity's evolution. Our desire to belong to such groups who share values, beliefs, goals, interests, or blood lines is steeped in our biology, our DNA. Yet the magnitude of wicked problems such as climate change, food insecurity, fundamentalist uprisings, and mass extinctions calls for us to cooperate in much larger groups than we have ever found necessary before. While it is in our innate nature to want to belong, it is paradoxically our desire to identify ourselves with small groups that is driving political polarisation, ongoing racism, and nationalism. When we embrace our unity, we can be at peace because finally there is no enemy to overcome—just a slightly altered mirror image of ourselves, perhaps like the ones we see at fun fairs. Maybe you disagree, and that's okay. For us to move from "me" to "we," fundamentalist or dogmatic views are not going to be helpful, and I try to hold my beliefs lightly. We don't necessarily need to agree; we just need to respect each other. We might look different, but we are all at our core human and each and every one of us is a citizen of this planet.

I believe we need to shift the collective narrative of who "we" are to incorporate much larger groups of people. My view is that Thatcher was wrong, society absolutely exists and we are absolutely entrenched within it. I can observe daily how my own life circumstances are intricately intertwined with the neighbours that live above and below my apartment, just as they are with the homeless elderly couple who say hello to my kids on our way to preschool every morning. The immigrant families who make the incredible Indian, Ethiopian, and Vietnamese food that I enjoy locally, and the woman who comes to clean my office late at night once everyone's gone home. We are dependent upon each other in so many ways. We now live in a globalised world; consequently, our greatest challenges are shared globally, and we have a responsibility to cooperate globally to solve them. We need much more collective ways of thinking and acting. I'm sure at this stage you're thinking, *Well, that's easy for you to say, but how do we do that with so many diverse interests, perspectives, and different belief systems?*

Let's return to story. Every now and then a story is so powerful that it unifies massive groups of people who were previously apart. We saw it in New Zealand in 2019 when virtually the whole country showed their support for the Muslim community in the wake of the Christchurch mosque shootings. We saw in the early days of COVID-19, when Italians sang and played music for each other from balconies, while New Yorkers banged pots and pans together each evening in solidarity and support for healthcare workers. These stories gained headlines because of the magnitude of the events they were associated with, but small acts of *kindness, compassion,* and *unity* quietly unfold all over the world every day. Perhaps we are just so accustomed to negative news and focusing on division that we don't pay attention to them until a crisis comes along to completely disrupt the narratives underpinning our lives. Once the crisis has broken the illusion of separation and awakened us to our interdependence, it takes a concerted and conscious effort not to slip back into old patterns. We need to keep telling stories that highlight what is possible when we work together, using frames of *solidarity*, *helpfulness*, *love*, and *togetherness*. Stories of collective impact, stories of different cultures learning from each other, or stories of political foes coming together to achieve something against the odds can inspire and break the old narratives of conflict and polarisation. Stories that challenge stereotypes and harmful narratives of the "other" can highlight how much we all have in common. This mythic reframing of "we" doesn't just refer to those who are alive today. It includes all who have come before and those who will come after, many generations from now. It may also include the life on this planet that is not human, from which we have much to learn.

It's worth remembering the tale of the ants from the southwestern United States. As the story goes, if you can catch one hundred or so red fire ants that live in the southwestern desert and put them in a jar with one hundred of the large black ants from the same region, not much will happen. That is, until you shake the jar vigorously and dump them out onto the ground. After being shaken up, the two types of ant will fight each other to the death. The red ants think the black ants are the enemy, and the black ants think the red ants are the enemy, when the real enemy is the person who shook the jar. We are all players in the grand story of life, we are all ants in the jar. When assessing the big problems we're facing as a global society, we need to stop pointing fingers at the easy targets, and ask ourselves who or what is shaking the jar.

17

FROM TREE TO ME

Current narrative: *Having mastered tools and technologies to access natural resources, we should use them to further our own interests and growth.*
New myth: *Humans are nature; what we do to nature, we do to ourselves.*

As I was walking home with my son one evening shortly after he turned three, he asked me why the moon was following him. This is a typical developmental question that young children ask as they begin to orient themselves in the world. As kids, we are at the centre of our own world. Somewhere along the way, we learn that the world is much bigger than the tiny corner that we occupy, yet collectively the narrative of human centrality in the universe still prevails. It is one that frames trees, soil, minerals, animal life, and water bodies as resources that are there for our use, and ignores their role as elements of a whole, interconnected ecosystem. This wasn't so much of a problem when there were small pockets of us spread around the planet. But with a global population expected to reach almost 10 billion by 2050, we are taking far more than we are giving. We are in the midst of a sixth mass extinction of species, driven for the most part by human activity, and I believe that with our human intelligence comes a duty of care to keep things in equilibrium. Not just for our own survival, but because we are simply one part of a diverse and interconnected web of life.

The story of human superiority over other species is a deeply ingrained one for millions of people and the idea that we are part of nature may be challenging to adopt for some. We tend to think that we are at the top of the food chain, but every now and then something like a virus comes along to remind us that other entities have the power to tip the balance. The types of stories that can help to nurture and propagate the myth of *humans as nature* are becoming more accepted the world over. Many of us assume a supposed polarity between science and spirituality. But whether it's the fact that we exchange 98 percent of the atoms in our body with the world around us every year, or advances in the field of quantum physics that suggest that the behaviour of subatomic particles is influenced by the observer, science is now telling us what indigenous cultures have known for countless generations: everything is intricately connected. What we see and perceive around us as separate forms is simply the current arrangement of atoms, ever changing. Highlighting these observations can help us to understand that we are part of something much bigger and more mysterious than our current understanding of science can explain. Highlighting stories that connect climate change and environmental degradation to people who are directly affected on a daily basis, such as Pacific Islanders grappling with sea-level rise or subsistence farmers experiencing crop failures across Africa, can help us to realise how intricately human destinies are tied up in the natural world.

A participant in a narrative workshop I facilitated recently lamented the persisting narrative that people who work in the field of environment and sustainability are all hippies. We talked about how that narrative had come about, who drives it, and questioned just where along the way a sense of wonder, joy, and love for the natural world became a radical or fringe thing? Following my graduation from university, I took a job as a park ranger in my favourite place in the world, Tongariro National Park. It is the place I consider my spiritual home, a place to which many of my favourite childhood memories and stories are tied, and where Māori legends of feuding mountains spewing fire at each other eons ago run rich and deep in the land. The six months I spent up there wandering the tussock-strewn, desert landscapes daily and sharing stories with visitors from all over the world are among the happiest times of my life. Call me a hippie, but given that this period of deep connection with nature served as the jumping off point for a career featuring policy development, social enterprise, public speaking, software development, journalism, and helping to facilitate venture capital investment towards making positive change for people and the planet, then the world is full of hippies and it's probably a very good thing.

Wherever we can connect anecdotes of happy, thriving societies and fulfilled human lives with stories of environmental regeneration, ecosystem preservation, and connection with the natural world, we have an opportunity to start painting a narrative of humans as inherently part of nature. Our choice of words plays a huge role. Rather than talking about humans having *governance* or *jurisdiction* over natural landscapes, we can reframe it as a *responsibility* or *duty of care*. Frames of separation such as *uninhabited* or *vacant land* suggest that if humans are not there then nothing is. The term *natural resources* implies that the trees, water, and other gifts of nature are there purely for the taking. Alternative frames that serve to reinforce the narrative of human connection to nature include talking about *living systems, stewardship, resilience,* and *regeneration.* Wherever possible, our language should recognise the complexities and delicate dependencies at play, rather than attempting to simplify and reduce whole living systems to their constituent parts. This is the greatest challenge with communicating the nature of climate change, with its intricate causality and feedback loops between the world's oceans, forests, polar regions, soil biology, agricultural practices, and anthropogenic activity. Planetary Boundaries theory and its related framework of Doughnut Economics provide helpful models that outline tipping points and safe operating zones across a number of interconnected ecological indicators.[1,2] As such, they are gathering popularity as frameworks of reference for developing social, economic, and environmental policy. But given how much harm we have already done to the planet, and the fact that we've already crossed several tipping points, we need a better story about our responsibility to the natural world.

18

FROM SUSTAINABILITY TO REGENERATION

Current narrative: *Through sustainable use of resources we can see continued growth and prosperity.*
New myth: *We have a duty to regenerate and repair the harm we have already caused.*

IN OCTOBER 1987, A UN-ESTABLISHED COMMISSION RELEASED A report entitled "Our Common Future," which has become better known as the "Brundtland Report," named after the former Norwegian Prime Minister Gro Harlem Brundtland who headed the commission. The report first introduced the terms *sustainable development* and *sustainability* to highlight the interconnectedness between economic, social, and ecological processes. The foundation of this multi-dimensional concept of sustainable development was later popularised at the 1992 Earth Summit in Rio de Janeiro. Thirty years later most governments and many businesses have some sort of sustainability policies in place relating to the natural environment and humankind's relationship with it. In more recent years, however, another term has emerged that better captures the spirit of what is truly required of us to stabilise the planet's biosphere: *regeneration*.

Whereas *sustainability* suggests protecting the current state of the environment, *regeneration* recognises that many natural ecosystems are already destroyed or significantly damaged. Sustaining a dead or dying ecosystem is of little good; after decades or even centuries of human abuse, many of the Earth's natural systems need our immediate assistance to regenerate and become restored. In addition, our approach to achieving *sustainability* often means offsetting an environmental harm with a perceived equal environmental or economic benefit somewhere else. Being content with *sustainability* is what allows us to clear complex native forest ecosystems to make way for agricultural lands, and then offset our carbon losses by planting monocultural tree forests with ecological dead zones beneath them. On paper, these numbers might work out. But anyone who has walked through a monoculture of plantation forestry and noticed the stark lack of bird, animal, and other plant life in the understorey can tell you that these economically driven models are far from sustainable. To fix what we have broken, we need to have loftier goals that build upon the interconnectedness of all elements of a living system. If we are a part of nature, as offered in the previous chapter, then this is a no-brainer. Why wouldn't we want to make our surrounding environments and thus ourselves healthier?

The stories that can support a mass shifting of narrative towards regeneration include those of regenerative agriculture, the circular economy, revitalisation of economically deprived communities, and restoration of damaged ecosystems. After co-producing a multi-media content series on regenerative agriculture in New Zealand in 2020, and taking a deep dive into the world of permaculture, silviculture, holistic grazing, and organics, I gained a new understanding of what was possible through these methods of farming. It was a fascinating glimpse into how an industry that has collectively done a lot of environmental harm could be reoriented to be a force for environmental repair. The stories of landowners using regenerative practices and principles to turn around tired old farms with degraded soils after years of overreliance on synthetic fertilisers was a powerful motivator for others who had become disillusioned with modern, industrial agriculture. By far the most potent change, however, was not an environmental one, but a rapidly spreading shift in mindset. After being blamed for environmental pollution by urban folks for many years, farmers could see themselves as being recognised as part of the solution. The soil was becoming rich and healthy again, the grass roots long, insect and birdlife returned, and several farmers told me that they had rediscovered the joy of farming once more.

Our current economic systems are inherently *degenerative* and *extractive*, but opportunities for regeneration and development of the circular economy are everywhere in our throw-away culture. When it comes to producing and buying things, our current economies are overwhelmingly *linear*. We need a product, we buy it, we use it for its limited lifespan, and then we throw it away. The circular economy presents an alternative model based on three core principles: designing waste and pollution out of product development; keeping products and materials in use; and regenerating natural systems. The Edmund Hillary Fellowship (EHF) community includes entrepreneurs turning trash into biofuel, converting food-crop waste into high-value yarn and fashion products, and diverting excess medical products from landfill to be shipped overseas to communities in dire need of them. The key framing here is that not only are these solutions reducing waste in our societies, they are also creating useful products that would otherwise require new raw materials to produce. Not only are they *doing good*, but they are also resulting in *less harm* overall. They are building *resilience* into the systems where the anthropogenic collides with the natural. *Circular systems, cradle-to-cradle* product life cycles, *regeneration* over *sustainability*, and *genuine win-wins* in which nobody is exploited along the way are all frames that can help us to imagine new ways of meeting our needs on a finite planet. Regulations and incentives can help to make circular economies more feasible against the throw-away status quo, but we also need a widespread culture shift. In many ways, regeneration represents a mindset of stepping backwards in time, in pace of life, and in some cases, in the ratio of human labour to output. It harks back to a time when our grandmothers darned socks and mended shirts, when we returned glass milk bottles for refilling, and when everybody composted and grew their own vegetables. While we see a resurgence of these types of practices in recent years, to some, the idea of learning to live with less is a threat to their perception of *progress*. It may challenge our identity, our freedom to consume, and our ability to amass the things that for many have come to represent a successful and happy life. So let's take a look at how we can instil a new myth of what constitutes a happy life.

19

—————————————————————

FROM STUFF TO ENOUGH

Current narrative: *Buying and owning lots of stuff is the
mark of a successful and happy life.*
New myth: *The key to happiness is being content with
having enough.*

I HAVE A FAVOURITE COOKING POT AT HOME THAT IS STAMPED
with "Made in Yugoslavia" on the bottom. It is a good sign that
a product still in use was built to last when it was made in a
country that hasn't existed for thirty years. In fact, this pot is
over forty years old, as my mother bought it shortly after her
wedding in the late 1970s. It is still going strong and is my
faithful go-to for soups and pasta. Looking at the pots and pans
for sale in most homeware stores these days, it is hard to
imagine that many of them will still be usable, let alone going
strong in forty years' time.

At its foundation, the modern-day version of capitalism that we
find ourselves with today requires that we buy ever more
things. Consequently, in-built obsolescence is common and
products are no longer built to last. Our use of Gross Domestic

Product (GDP) as a measure of a nation's wellbeing and progress dictates that if a pot, a chair, a pair of shoes, or an iPhone breaks or ceases to be functional a few years after purchase and you need to buy another one, this is *a good thing*. Only in a world that still believes in what climate activist Greta Thunberg has called *"fairytales of eternal economic growth"* could this possibly be a good thing. Yet our global economic system is still rooted in the narrative that endless growth is not only possible, but desirable and commendable.

The notion is as farcical as it is pervasive. We have an overwhelming amount of evidence telling us that infinite growth is, indeed, not possible on a planet with finite resources. We need only look at the state of our oceans, freshwater bodies, and dwindling rainforests to understand this, but we collectively behave as if it is true. This illustrates the subconscious power of our prevailing economic narratives and of those who seek to perpetuate them, along with the sense of inertia we feel at the enormity of the challenge. Even promises of a techno-utopian future where technology will solve our problems and herald a new age of prosperity for all is a red herring if we are still following the narrative that more equals better. The urge to satiate our desire for buying things is exacerbated by an advertising industry that plays on our fears and sense of lack. Here we see that the myth of endless growth is interdependent on another narrative—the one that says that buying stuff will make you happy. It is a story that holds great power over the human race. If you have a problem or feel unsatisfied, you buy a thing you think you need and you feel happy. At least for a little while. And once you're sad again or face another problem, just rinse and repeat. This message is not accidental; it is core to the success of marketing departments the world over, in order to increase profits and revenues and keep our economies afloat.

The viewpoint that capitalism is broken is a much more acceptable one today than it was twenty or even ten years ago. So the challenge now is to encourage collective adherence to a new myth of what it means to be happy, and a new definition of progress. Tales of sudden epiphanies, life transformations, and everyday people finding peace and enjoyment in the simple things in life are among those that can help shift the dial away from narratives that link consumerism, happiness, and economic growth. We find inspiration in the stories of people who have lost everything they own and emerged out the other side transformed. They illustrate a deep human truth about what really makes us happy, and it seldom has much to do with the balance of our bank account. The predominant frame of this new mythology is that many of us do in fact have *enough*.

Of course, there are many people living in genuine poverty and I'm not referring to these folks with this sweeping generalisation. Having enough money to afford a decent quality of life, a warm roof over your head, food on the table, and a little extra for the odd luxury is certainly linked to happiness. But beyond a comfortable income, more money doesn't make you happier. Research conducted in 2018 suggests that levels of happiness stop rising alongside income at between US$60,000 and $95,000 per year depending on region of the world, while life satisfaction peaked at an income of US$105,000 in the United States.[1]

It's a tall order to transcend the bombardment of advertising that encourages us to buy ever more stuff, but it starts with framing a happy life in terms of our intrinsic values. Looking at the big picture is also helpful for focusing on the problem rather than the person. How often do we hear that a person or a company is *greedy*? It's a common frame but is one that singles out one individual or company that is merely operating within a broken economic and cultural system. After all, that "greedy" person is only doing what society tells us is right and good. An alternative to referring to someone as greedy might be to point out *how easily money corrupts*. This places the problem with money itself and our cultural relationship to it. We can talk about *what brings us joy*. Highlighting one example, we can start questioning why it is still culturally celebrated as a mark of success to make money by investing heavily in real estate when in many countries hardworking people in their forties on a good income still can't afford to buy a first home. At time of writing in mid-2021, average house prices in New Zealand have reached NZ$943,000 (roughly US$660,000), thanks in part to decades of policy inaction on affordable housing and widespread property investment from those who have capital to leverage. We can begin to frame such non-productive investments as *land hoarding*, and the economic policies that encourage it as *socially irresponsible, perverse incentives* that are *driving inequality*.

The question at the core of any economic transformation is: What is the purpose of the economy? Is it economic growth for the sake of it? Or is it rather that *growth* has become a proxy for some other goal? The etymology of the word *wealth* has some telling origins. The word comes from the old English *weal*, which means "welfare and wellbeing." *Weal* is in turn related to the older world *wel*, meaning "in a state of good fortune, welfare, and happiness." By the fifteenth century, the meaning of the word had become much more akin to what we commonly understand as wealth today, associated with material riches and financial prosperity. What if we were to reframe our understanding of *wealth* to its original meaning, and in doing so reframe the purpose of the economy? What would it mean for nations to strive to make all their citizens rich in happiness and wellbeing?

Bhutan has received much attention and accolades for its Gross National Happiness Index, enacted in 2008. Several other alternatives to Gross Domestic Product (GDP) have emerged in recent years including the OECD's Better Life Index and the UN's Human Development Index. In 2019, New Zealand launched its first Wellbeing Budget, and since 2011, the country's Treasury has been developing a Living Standards Framework that focuses on promoting higher standards of living and greater intergenerational wellbeing. Inherent in the framework is a recognition that the country's four broad types of capital—natural, social, human, and financial/physical capital—need to each be strong in their own right and to support each other. This reframing of our traditional, narrow understanding of the concept of capital and how it relates to the wellbeing of a nation provides the nuance, perspective, and balance that GDP cannot.

The question of what will replace today's version of capitalism is a complex one, and I certainly don't have all the answers. But whatever it will be, it will be a smoother transition if more of us believe in a narrative of happiness that is grounded in non-material things. Inspiration can be found in models such as Kate Raworth's Doughnut Economics, which suggests that a safe and just economy exists between a social foundation of wellbeing for all, and an ecological ceiling above which we are degrading the planet beyond repair.[2] We are currently sitting outside the doughnut and we need to get back inside it. In part that will mean rethinking the global mechanisms of supply and demand that underpin our understanding of scarcity and abundance.

20

FROM SCARCITY TO ABUNDANCE

Current narrative: *Resources are scarce and there is not enough to go around.*
New myth: *With the right systems in place, our lives can be full of abundance.*

EVERY YEAR, WE HEAR THE COMMON REFRAIN: WE NEED TO GROW more food to feed a rapidly growing global population. In 2009, the UN announced that global food production would have to double by 2050 to meet the world's demands.[1] Then in 2012, the World Wildlife Federation suggested that we would need to produce as much food in the following forty years as humanity has in the last eight thousand years.[2] Despite the UN figure being challenged as an overestimation, it is the figure that is frequently used by food industry giants and heavily lobbied governments alike as a justification for an expansion of industrial agriculture. While there is truth to the narrative—we are indeed looking down the barrel of a rapidly growing global population that will need to be fed—the story is incomplete. A point that is frequently missing from the conversations about needing to drastically scale production and feed the world is the fact that roughly one third of food produced is wasted every year.[3] About 28 percent of the world's agricultural land is being used to produce food that feeds absolutely no one. If this in itself is not tragedy enough, the associated greenhouse gas emissions, energy and freshwater use, loss of top soil, and chemical fertiliser used to grow that food was all for nothing. When we speak of food scarcity, seldom do we pause to think about whether it is really an issue of supply or rather a complex mix of challenges relating to supply chain distribution, market forces, transportation challenges, regulatory barriers, and culture surrounding food. Grocery stores, for example, regularly reject fruits and vegetables if they don't meet market-based quality standards around shape, size, colour, and level of ripeness. If the current market price for a crop is too low, farmers may let it rot in the fields as the labour costs for harvesting and transportation outweigh the revenues. This is not real scarcity, it is *manufactured scarcity*, the product of a human-designed economic system.

The narrative of needing to drastically increase food production also rarely focuses on what sort of food we are producing, where we are producing it, and what we are doing with it. Many Western diets include large amounts of heavily processed foods that are reliant on vast amounts of land, resources, and energy for raw ingredient production. These products are not so much food in the sense that our great-grandmothers would recognise them as such. They are rather foodstuffs that lack in nutrition and are laden with salt, sugar, and preservatives that contribute to a whole array of modern-day health issues. We then ship these same foodstuffs, along with luxury goods that are out of season, thousands of miles around the globe. We have a cultural narrative of consumer choice that suggests there is nothing wrong with eating fresh strawberries from the other side of the world in the middle of winter, no matter what the environmental and economic cost. Local food movements are growing in popularity, and these are providing different stories about food that focus on healthier, in-season produce. Stories that highlight local food and beverage production can also strike a chord, connecting people to place. Framing things in terms of *sustenance*, *nutrition*, and *food equality* rather than just total *food produced* can be helpful in helping us to rethink food scarcity.

The narrative of scarcity is core to the functioning of capitalism as we known it. The pursuit of growth, profit, and productivity are all rooted in a mindset of there *never being enough*. It is the narrative that tells us there is simply not enough to go around, or at least not for everyone to live in a state of comfort, and therefore we must put a fair price on resources to keep things in balance. But if we are to take the global food issue as an example, the problem is not so much one of production, but of distribution. It's not that there isn't enough food, it's just in the wrong place at the wrong time. It is market forces, geopolitical boundaries, trade barriers, and cultural attitudes towards the exchange of value that are the drivers of food wastage. And thus the issue is not just one of agricultural production, but also a social and political problem. We need to be sure that we are not equating *scarcity* with *inequitable resource distribution*. Our biosphere cannot sustain the industrial agricultural expansion necessary to grow more food without drastically changing the adjacent systems. Framing things to shine a light on these seldom-spoken truths can help us to overcome a culture rooted in the notion of scarcity, and to start thinking about how we can increase abundance.

I have used food as an example so far, but the same patterns are true for many other products that suffer from false scarcity. Save fossil fuels and some rare-earth minerals, most of the resources that we consider to be scarce could be much more abundant if we would only build our anthropogenic systems around the notions of equitable distribution, regeneration, and circular economies. Energy is abundant if we derive it from natural sources such as wind and solar. The entire world's energy needs could be met by capturing the sunlight that shines on just 1.2% of the Sahara Desert each year.[4] The challenge would be in distribution obviously, but framing it in such terms certainly helps us to understand just how abundant energy really is. Fresh water could be abundant if we were to treat it as the gift and human right that it truly is, rather than as a commodity. Decent jobs and financial comfort could be abundant if we were to place due value on undervalued vocations such as caregiving, teaching, social work, and nursing. Even the rare-earth minerals such as neodymium, terbium, and dysprosium that make our smartphones vibrate would be less scarce if we were to put in place incentives and mandates for better phone-recycling systems. We can choose to talk not of *scarcity*, but to instead frame the solutions as finding ways to improve the *availability*, *accessibility*, and *distribution* of resources; when talking about global inequalities in resource distribution and access, be it in food, water, education, or finance, reframing things in terms of *fairness*, *equality*, *equity*, and *human rights* can be helpful. From there, we can place *sovereignty*, *self-determination*, and *partnership* at the centre of conversations about addressing hunger and poverty in developing nations, instead of *aid*, or of *helping* or *saving* people.

21

FROM COMPETITION TO COLLABORATION

Current narrative: *Competition is the best way to drive innovation to solve problems.*
New myth: *When we work together, anything is possible.*

IN THE EARLY 1970S RICHARD STALLMAN WAS PART OF A community of hackers at the MIT Artificial Intelligence Laboratory. Back then the term "hackers" didn't have the same negative connotations that it does today surrounding ransomware and the theft of data, but rather referred to those who liked to get into the guts of a system, tinker with it, and make it better. Driven by an anti-establishment attitude and a willingness to cooperate with other programmers, Richard was a vocal critic of restricted computer access, and at one point decrypted the passwords introduced by MIT's Laboratory for Computer Science, helping students to regain anonymous access to the system. He would eventually go on to launch the free software movement and pioneer the concept of "copyleft" —the practice of granting the right to freely distribute and modify intellectual property within certain parameters. Both were precursors to the open source software movement, which has seen unimaginable gains in efficiency in software development over the past few decades through the practice of sharing and iterating on source code. The fundamental premise behind Richard's work, and the work of countless open source advocates out there today, is that we can achieve so much more when we collaborate, share our learnings, and avoid mistakes that others have already made. While his views might have been radical, the collaborative spirit that he nurtured provides a great deal of inspiration for how we might work together to tackle complex global problems in the future. It is the antithesis to the idea that competition is necessary to drive innovation.

Turning to a starkly different story, small-scale Indigenous farmers in the Andean highlands of Bolivia and Peru have cultivated quinoa to feed their families for thousands of years. Long scorned by urban-dwelling Bolivians as the food of poor people, all that changed around the late 2000s when the West discovered the nutritional value of quinoa, which boasts a high protein content and all nine essential amino acids. Over the last ten years, this humble seed has grown significantly in popularity and along with its rise, the price has shot up and production has increased massively. Large commercial growers nearer to the coast have been able to out-price family farmers in the highlands, undercutting their profits, while the relative price hike has meant this staple food is often too expensive for the locals to eat. Through competitive market forces not of their own making, a crop that has been a staple for over three thousand years has gone from abundance to being scarce for the people of the Andes. A somewhat similar situation unfolded in Mexico after the North American Free Trade Agreement (NAFTA) was signed, and US-imported corn flooded the market. Mexican farmers couldn't compete with US-government-subsidised corn farmers to the north and within the first decade of NAFTA, Mexican corn prices fell by 66 percent.[1] What was pitched as "healthy competition" destroyed many millions of livelihoods, and fuelled the impoverishment of one economy to the benefit of another. It also contributed to an increase of undocumented Mexican immigrants heading across the border in search of a better life.

Over the past few hundred years, a culture of competition in business has served us well in many regards. It has encouraged outside-the-box thinking and, in some cases, has helped us avoid monopolies that keep consumer prices high. In the past when governments' ability to regulate was much stronger than it is today, healthy competition spawned new industries and technologies that improved our lives drastically. But today, when we are facing a growing population, overconsumption, and the privatisation of key government functions, alongside the collapse of various parts of the biosphere, climate refugees, looming water wars, and increasing social unrest, perhaps it's time to rethink whether a competitive mindset is the best strategy for our global economy going forward. A protectionist approach towards ideas and technologies in the form of intellectual property is hampering our ability to solve some of the biggest challenges that humanity faces. Tesla made waves in 2014 when it announced it was making all its patents freely available in order to accelerate the development of the electric vehicle market. Imagine if manufacturers and producers took a similar approach to clean energy, infrastructure, biomass gasification, data, and food production. How much more efficient could governments and businesses be if they weren't hiring pricey consultants to build software from scratch every time they needed a new platform or digital service? We could accelerate innovation rapidly, develop new products and solutions, and drive down prices for consumers, helping to level out the inequality gap.

The free and open source software movements have paved the way for many offshoots with the same core fundamental belief: we are better when we work together. Open data, open government, peer-to-peer exchange systems, and money-free markets are all providing collaborative alternatives to the competition mindset that dominates our exchange of products and services. It might seem naive to think that these systems are going to replace the fundamental capitalist ideal that the market knows best. It might also seem naive to assume that large corporations with patents should be more interested in levelling out inequality than increasing shareholder value (and indeed in some places, they are legally bound to the latter). But the more we can start believing in the new myths covered in the previous two chapters, surrounding the notions of abundance and having enough, the more appealing and practical these solutions will seem. If we start shifting narratives of what makes us happy, and realise that we have so much more to work with when we reuse and pool resources, we might discover that we don't need as much money to live as we think we do. More and more countries are exploring forms of universal basic income and many communities are experimenting with alternatives to monetary exchange such as time-banking, skills sharing, and resource sharing. These alternatives represent a value exchange that is *relational* in nature, rather than *transactional*. Joining and nurturing decentralised, collaborative networks like Enspiral can help redefine the narratives underpinning the ways in which we support each other in our work.

Stories that highlight how much time, energy, and resources are wasted by unnecessary re-inventing of the wheel can help us to realise how ridiculous parts of our economic system have become. The term *freedom* means a lot of different things to different people, and there is a great deal of dissonance between the different interpretations. The question at the centre of the debate is *Whose freedom and at what costs? Free trade* agreements have served to strengthen the economic might of ruling superpowers more than anyone, and while smaller, less affluent nations have seen some improvements in quality of life, they have also experienced an erosion of many of their local markets resulting in millions of job losses. *Free trade* isn't *free*, it's just an *externalisation of costs* to poorer populations and their environments, and as such it's an unhelpful term to use. As we move more from *we* to *me*, we may begin to see just how much free trade agreements have had harmful effects on people, in both rich and poor countries. Meanwhile, framing the fruits of collaborative efforts as *win-wins*, *improving efficiency*, and *driving innovation* can help with uptake from sectors of society who are dubious of a move away from competition. Who knows, if we work together and avoid duplication of efforts, we might even find we have more time in our lives to rest, relax, and recharge.

22

FROM HUMAN DOINGS TO HUMAN BEINGS

Current narrative: *We need to be constantly busy and more productive to be successful and get ahead in life.*
New myth: *There are times for doing, and times for not doing.*

Towards the final stages of writing this book, I spent half an hour of my thirty-ninth birthday sitting at an outside table in a local bar and café waiting for a friend who was running late. As an experiment, I attempted to do nothing but sit and watch the world go by until she arrived. Even with such a level of intentionality, I found that I was only able to sit doing nothing for a couple of minutes at a time, before picking up my phone to do something. I would reply to a message, check the weather forecast, or check my schedule for the following day. In fact, I'm writing these very words on my phone as I sit waiting. Many of us are so accustomed to being *productive* and *achieving* things, ticking chores off our list, that we find it difficult to just sit, be, and observe.

Building on the previous chapter, the prevailing narrative of productivity is closely linked to our cultural elevation of a competitive economy. It is one that urges us to work ever longer hours, be on call 24/7, and to prioritise work above family, leisure time, and creative pursuits. Combined with a mindset of scarcity and competition, the narrative dictates, "If you're not getting ahead, someone else is." Have you ever found yourself reading a blog post on productivity tips instead of actually doing the work you are supposed to be doing? I know I have. The more fervent of us are driven to hack our productive time, installing apps, and learning new tips and tricks. Productivity in and of itself is not the problem; it is not necessarily a bad thing to work smarter and do more with less investment of time, resources, or people power. But when the term *productive* becomes synonymous with *greater economic gain* as it has in many economies, we are valuing only one aspect of our human purpose—that which we can *create*, *produce*, or *do*. We relegate our worth to that of "human doings" rather than "human beings," reducing real lives to the value of the outputs that we can produce.

I facilitated a narrative workshop where a participant wanted to disrupt the narrative that you need to be busy to be successful. We place so much value on the work of producing or creating something that it becomes a badge of honour to be busy and tired. In Japan, it is so common that people literally work themselves to death that there is a word for it: *karoshi*. Whether the pressure is coming from the office or from a desire to be connected via social media, the need to be constantly available on our phones is making many of us anxious and keeping our stress response systems in overdrive. The World Health Organization has gone as far as to label stress the "health epidemic of the 21st century." It is slowly becoming more acceptable and even encouraged in some circles that we should regularly spend time resting, relaxing, observing life go by, and enjoying time with the people we love. There is a growing recognition that these periods of non-doing are beneficial to our mental health.

Stories of those who are taking time off work to spend more time with their children or focus on a passion project can inspire others to redefine the narrative of productivity for themselves. In saying that, I want to acknowledge that it is a privilege to have the choice to spend less time working and more time with family. Within our current economic system, spending less time earning money is not an option for a great proportion of the population. But other ways of practising presence are accessible to anyone. We can all choose to put our phones down when we don't have any particular purpose or task in mind for them. By observing and talking with people face to face, we can learn more about real human beings rather than carefully cultivated online personas. We can choose to view doing as a means to an end, and stop when we are finished with a particular task, rather than feeling the need to constantly achieve more. It's a lesson I am constantly learning (and not always successfully). Questioning what brings us *contentment*, *presence*, *enjoyment*, and *fulfilment* can help us determine what activities bring us joy and benefit our mental health. Within organisations we can stop talking about *outputs* and *KPIs* (key performance indicators), and instead focus on *outcomes* and *milestones*.

I think we also need to take a good look and redefine what sort of activities we typically value as productive in our societies. It is commonplace for us to think of productivity in terms of what we can achieve in our work and organisational life. It is less common to hear of productivity in reference to the work of raising children, helping others in the community, reading, planting trees, exercising, meditating, or just mucking around with a new hobby. These are all legitimate investments into our future and into moulding multi-dimensional human beings with *happy, fulfilled lives*. If this is the true purpose of the economy, as I have previously suggested, then these things are absolutely productive activities. We have all heard stories of people who have had a near-death experience, a health scare, or some other sort of disruption that jolted them out of the relentless pursuit of some idea of future happiness, and caused them to start living in the now. But we can't manufacture these experiences. The reality is that most of us need to learn how to slow down and enjoy life the good old-fashioned way—by watching our brains, noticing when they are busy, and becoming more conscious of when we are acting out of an automatic or habitual response, like picking up our phone with no particular purpose in mind. Intentionality helps us to become better at doing things when we need or choose to, and then at just being when nothing particularly needs to be done. We may just find ourselves experiencing the benefits of great insight that often come out of times of silence and stillness.

One bonus of allowing for more time in our lives that isn't productive, in the traditional sense of the word, is having the space to grieve that which we are losing and that which is already lost. Much of what I am suggesting with these ten new myths for humanity is a substantial deviation from the narratives that have come to underpin our lives. Additionally, we are living in an era of accelerating change. In times of great upheaval when our narratives are challenged, whether personal or collective, it is normal and common to grieve what was or will become lost. After all, these narratives are familiar. They bring us comfort and stability, a story of the world that is unshakable. They inform the decisions we make, they shape our identity, they influence the ways in which we spend our time, money, and mental energy. Even when we are shedding narratives that we have come to realise are no longer serving us well, it is natural to feel unsettled about it. Just as Stockholm syndrome has hostage victims hesitant to leave the clutches of those who have held them captive, our familiarity with the old stories and the ways in which we have gone about our lives exerts a power over us that is difficult to resist. Transitions are hard, and we need to make space to sit with the discomfort that they bring. While we are grieving the changes in the narratives that guide our lives, we might also find the time to acknowledge and reconcile what it is that we have collectively done to our planet, the species that call it home, our oceans, our atmosphere, and our fellow humans. There is little point wallowing in guilt about these regrettable realities; to a large extent, guilt is not a useful emotion. But we can choose to grieve the species that have gone extinct under our watch, the languages lost, the thousands of varieties of fruits and vegetables that are gone forever, and the loss of our collective innocence. After the grieving, we may move forwards towards redemption. From there we can build a healthy relationship with the future that is grounded in a sense of agency to right our wrongs and do things differently in the future, rather than feelings of guilt and grief. To do this, we must allow the time and space to go through the motions of grieving, be kind and patient to ourselves and others, and to feel what we need to feel in order to move out the other side.

23

FROM WEST TO THE REST

Current narrative: *Western civilised thought is superior to other more primitive belief systems.*
New myth: *Knowledge comes in many legitimate ways, forms, and methodologies.*

SCROLLING THROUGH SOCIAL MEDIA ONE DAY, I SAW A BRILLIANT meme that captured the predominant "West is best" narrative of defining and solving problems. Picturing a group of African children standing upon a rock and looking out upon a grand vista of natural savanna beauty, one of the children was portrayed in a speech bubble as saying, "Do you know that in America children are forced to stay inside and sit down all day to learn about the world, and when they get too energetic or excited they are given drugs to make them calm down?" Another child responds, "Wow, that's terrible. We should take up a collection for them."

In an instant, this meme said so much. It challenged not just our approach to aid and development, and the inherent assumptions about what people in other countries might need, but also took aim at problematic aspects of Western education systems and healthcare responses to dealing with childhood conditions surrounding attention and hyperactivity. The international aid and development sector is littered with abandoned projects that were rolled out with good intentions, yet failed to understand the cultural narratives and norms that underpinned the communities they were seeking to change. This phenomenon, grounded in the story of the *white saviour*, assumes that those in Western countries with higher levels of economic development and formal education know better than those in less economically developed countries. The narrative that science and empirical data is the gold standard of knowledge has largely gone unquestioned for a long time, and those who do question it risk becoming marginalised. Indigenous ways of knowing have been scoffed at for generations, with coordinated efforts to "educate" and re-programme the minds of Indigenous people towards Western mindsets and "civilised" ways of thinking and behaving. But in all our cleverness, we have split the world up into singular, narrow, constituent parts to the point where we need to be reminded of a most fundamental truth: the world is made up of intricate systems and that everything is interconnected.

Our prevailing narrative that Western powers know better has also provided us with the justification to do some terrible things with the excuse that we are the right ones, the civilised people, the good guys. The indoctrination of Western thinking and forced removal of Indigenous children from their families and communities in Canada, the United States, Australia, and New Zealand comes to mind. The systematic eradication of indigenous languages has resulted in a massive loss to our cultural heritage. I have also often marvelled at the absurdity and hypocrisy of Western governments and media (and particularly the American media) reporting on the possibility of harboured weapons of mass destruction in other countries, while making no mention at all of the fact that the United States itself harbours the second highest number of nuclear weapons in the world after Russia. The US holds the additional dishonour of being the only country in the history of the world to have ever used nuclear weapons in combat. The underlying narrative excusing the stockpiling and deployment of nuclear arms by the US is that it is a democratic state where there are checks and balances on those in power. The subtext is that American leaders are responsible, rational, and trustworthy, while leaders of states like North Korea and Iraq are unhinged, corrupt, or too unbalanced to hold the responsibility of having nuclear weapons. Whatever truth there may be in these underlying narratives, the fact remains that America has twice proven itself the most irresponsible country on Earth when it comes to weapons of mass destruction. The direction of US politics in recent years also raises questions about the integrity of its narrative as a free and democratic state.

The process of decolonising our minds begins with recognising that Western models of thinking can only take us so far, and in some instances they have taken us entirely in the wrong direction. In this time of global upheaval and uncertainty, stories that inspire and ground us in our innate humanity are helpful. In many cases, we can take our inspiration from non-Western and indigenous cultures and look to their stories and myths for guidance. Not to unduly glorify, romanticise, or to co-opt, but to give credit where credit is due and take encouragement that *collectivism, community, ritual,* and a *sense of belonging* can be a healing tonic to the feeling of disconnection that many of us experience. Stories that are ripe with myth, analogy, and allegory hold fundamental truths that can connect us to something larger than ourselves, whatever we might perceive that something to be. Indigenous cultures don't need to be reminded that the world is made up of systems and everything is connected. They don't *think* it; they *know* and *feel* it. We can gain a lot from embracing frames of uncertainty and mystery, and abandoning our need for absolute clarity. We do not need to reject science in order to do this, and let me be clear that I am not advocating that we do so. Scientific progress has improved the lives of billions and certainly has its place in helping us better understand the nature of the complex problems we are facing. But I believe that we also need to learn how to be okay with ambiguity, or question the helpfulness of dualistic or reductionist thinking in situations when it is hampering our ability to think laterally. In the complex world in which we live, and particularly when it comes to changing systems, multiple and supposedly conflicting things can be true at once. It requires a certain degree of *humility* and *grace* to be open to *not knowing*, and this way of thinking is not yet welcome in most of our organisations, our media networks, and certainly not within our governments. But we can start with ourselves, share our own stories about embracing complexity and ambiguity, and highlight the stories of others who are walking similar paths. We can start with the mantra to not believe everything we think. I recognise that this can be shaky territory, particularly in a time when fake news, disinformation, and conspiracy theories are reaching epidemic proportions. With many different interests vying for attention and for their version of truth to be heard, we need to walk a fine line between trusting expert knowledge and acknowledging that many legitimate knowledge systems have long gone unheeded. We need to avoid being hasty about jumping to conclusions or following linear trains of thought when we're dealing with non-linear challenges. A move towards improving our adoption of complex systems science and transdisciplinary research methods, which allow for multiple lines of inquiry, is a step in the right direction. We cannot solve our problems with the same kind of reductionist thinking that created them in the first place. While Western knowledge systems have provided us with much, we must somehow make way for other legitimate forms of knowledge that are harder to objectively measure, such as feeling, sensing, and intuiting.

24

FROM MANKIND TO HUMANKIND

Current narrative: *It's a man's world, and patriarchal social and political structures are best.*
New myth: *The gifts and approaches of all genders hold value.*

THERE IS AN ELEPHANT IN THE ROOM OF EVERYTHING I'VE TALKED about so far in this final section. All of the preceding new myths and narrative shifts that I have outlined in the previous chapters will be impossible to achieve without restructuring our workplaces, homes, communities, and governments to more evenly distribute power and responsibility across all genders. It's all well and good to say that we should regenerate the land and our communities, or that we should take more time off work to spend time with the kids, but if this work always falls on women while the men continue to go on business-as-usual and do the "real work," then we are only serving to perpetuate unequal distributions of wealth and power. When it comes to collectivism vs individualism, women have generally been carrying more of the "we" than the "me" for a long time. Women have likewise been afforded fewer opportunities to rise up within workplaces or in scientific communities where intellectual thinking is valued. The situation for transgender and gender non-binary folks is even worse.

To be honest, it took me a long time to become comfortable with using the term "patriarchy," given how loaded it is with connotations of man-hating feminists shouting in the street. Not that there is anything wrong with feminism or shouting in the street, I've certainly been involved in my fair share of both. But as I have gained a more nuanced understanding of just how pervasive the unspoken assumptions of male supremacy are in our culture, I have come to realise just how deeply they affect everything from advertising and corporate decision-making, to healthcare and even queer culture. *Patriarchy* can be loosely defined as a social system in which men are the primary holders of power, enjoying supremacy and social privilege in politics, workplaces, moral matters, money, and the ownership of property. In some cultures it is overt, where there is a strict gender hierarchy and clearly defined roles and responsibilities for men and women. Often these structures have their roots in religious institutions and dogma, which throughout history have also been overwhelmingly controlled by men. In other cultures, rights and privileges are more equal at least in name, yet many of us are living under a guise of gender equality. Policies are put in place with good intention that prohibit discrimination based on gender, but the subtleties and nuances embedded in the culture have yet to catch up. The systems built by mankind have yet to transition to the systems of humankind. The longer we take to tip the scales to be more equal, the longer we are collectively depriving ourselves of the emotional and intellectual gifts, contributions, and approaches of over half of the world's population.

Notwithstanding the fact that men gain a lot from systems of patriarchal dominance, they are not immune to the toxic effects as well. Young boys and men are under immense pressure to behave in ways that are culturally understood to be "masculine"—in many cultures that means being confident and assertive, never showing fear, and suppressing emotion lest they be seen to be weak or "feminine." Young children are expected to behave in certain gendered ways from an early age. We need only to look to any given schoolyard and hear the taunt that a young boy runs or throws like a girl. As adults, men carry trauma and suppressed pain out into the world, which perpetuates gender division as they perceive a need to hold on to power. The truth is that patriarchal systems are doing us all a great deal of harm.

We can go a long way towards a new myth of valuing all genders by simply recognising the norm of maleness in our societies. Gender inequality is built into the very foundations of our societies. Patriarchal language that is largely second nature controls the stories, the beliefs, and the mythologies of our culture, embedding conflict, aggression, coercion, dominance, and competition into our psyche. Gender is often invisible when we dissect or discuss both problems and solutions. Have you ever heard a reporter or journalist who is reporting on a terrorist attack point out the fact that a terrorist is male? There is always plenty of focus to find out if their motives were rooted in fundamentalist religious doctrine. But unless there is a clear link such as in the case of mass shooters who identify themselves as incels (involuntary celibate men who believe that women owe them sex), we rarely stop to think about how their motives are rooted in patriarchal doctrine. We neglect to dissect and question why it is that the vast majority of terrorists are male. The invisible norm of maleness is highlighted by the fact that air-conditioning settings in many offices are set to the metabolism of the average male and that women employees consequently find it too cold. Women's versions of products such as razors frequently cost more than the men's version despite being identical aside from colour or branding, a phenomenon that has come to be known as the "pink tax." Patriarchal narratives dictate our cultural understanding of how girls and women "should" act and present themselves, by wearing makeup, smiling constantly, and taking unsolicited catcalls or harassment as a compliment that they have somehow passed the test to be considered attractive by a man. These ingrained narratives encourage tabloid media to dissect the choice of dress for a female celebrity or politician, while completely ignoring the clothes of their male counterparts. They are the reason we devalue jobs traditionally held by women such as nursing, childcare, and caring for the disabled, and they enable the gender wage gap to persist even in seemingly progressive and forward-thinking organisations, institutions, and nations.

To create social systems of true gender equality, we need to carefully examine the ways in which we may be subtly reinforcing gender stereotypes and expectations in all our communications and storytelling. Any stories that disrupt gender norms, highlight the achievements of women, or use frames that celebrate and normalise traits that are culturally understood as "feminine" can be helpful. Historically, "masculine" traits of *dominance* and *control* are associated with leadership, but the world's media made much of the *kindness* and *compassion* displayed by New Zealand Prime Minister Jacinda Ardern in the wake of the Christchurch mosque shootings. It was a refreshing change from the forceful rhetoric we usually see in the wake of terrorist attacks, and her behaviour was held up as an example for other world leaders to follow. I refer to "masculine" and "feminine" traits in quotation marks because of their predominant association with gender, but members of any gender can embody any of these traits. There is no good reason kindness, connection, and nurturance shouldn't be human traits, and indeed a great number of men around the world are actively working towards dismantling toxic narratives surrounding what it means to be "masculine."

It need not always be heavy. We've seen Disney taking positive steps in recent years with the relational focus of *Frozen* being the act of true love between siblings Elsa and Anna. In a stark deviation from previous Disney plot arcs focused on the romantic finale, Anna turns away from the man she loves to save her sister. Stories that position women as *strong* and *capable* are generally more helpful than those that paint women as victims, although these stories also have their place in highlighting inequalities and gender-based violence. Empowering and educating women is a significant lever to pull to improve economic conditions in less affluent nations. Nungshi and Tashi Malik are two sisters who are changing the narrative of what young women in India can achieve, through adventure racing and mountaineering. They are the first set of twins to summit the highest peaks of each of the world's seven continents and reach both the South and North Poles. Upon reaching the summit of Mount Vinson in Antarctica, the sisters banged a spoon upon a stainless-steel plate—a ritual that is traditionally performed to announce the birth of a newborn boy in their home state of Haryana, India. Newborn baby girls receive no such welcome, and in their mountain-top stunt the twins sought to send a message to the world that girls and their achievements should be celebrated too.

The more we send messages that disrupt gender norms, the faster we will make progress and it's never too early to begin. Children's stories are a great place to start for younger audiences. The stories that tell little boys that they can be vulnerable and little girls that they can build, climb, and be messy can help encourage young people that they are not limited by the narratives surrounding their gender. We can strive to embed values and qualities of *tenacity* and *compassion* into children in equal measure to form better-rounded individuals, organisations, and communities. Small children are paying attention and taking their cues from us far earlier than we think. And to be clear, this is not about women taking over the world from men; it's about shifting the stories we tell and assume to be true surrounding gender, and placing value on the approaches and contributions provided by all genders.

25

FROM NOW TO FOREVERMORE

Current narrative: *Life is short, enjoy it while you can.*
New myth: *We are but a tiny speck in the history of
humankind, and there are many generations to come.*

IN THE SOUTHERN HEMISPHERE SPRING OF 2020, MY WIFE AND I
took a stroll along Wellington's Oriental Bay coastline. Each
wearing our own set of headphones, we must have made for a
strange sight—two people clearly walking together yet
seemingly ignoring each other. But unbeknownst to passersby,
we were experiencing something rather magical together. We
had each downloaded an app called the Deep Time Walk onto
our phones, and had synced the soundtracks as we walked
simultaneously down the parade. Together we walked for 4.6
km, as two narrators took us through the 4.6-billion-year
history of the Earth. Each hundred metres we walked
accounted for a hundred million years. For the longest time at
the beginning, not much happened. Multi-cellular life entered
the picture at about 1.8 billion years before present, and it
wasn't until 385 million years ago—or 38.5 metres—that trees
entered the picture. The final segment saw plant life

proliferating, dinosaurs came and went, and finally in the last 20 centimetres of the walk, humans entered the picture. Ponder that for a moment: out of 4.6 km representing the history of this planet just 20 centimetres, about the length of the average handspan, represented the 200,000 years or so that human beings have been around. For most of our short history on this Earth, humans had very little effect in the grand scheme of things. And then in the last 250 years, which in the Deep Time Walk app would have represented roughly the length of a dust mite, we have managed to completely destabilise the oceans, forests, soils, land-based ecosystems, and climatic system of an entire planet, seeing hundreds of plant and animal species going extinct in the process. It's a sobering thought when you realise just how long this planet has been here.

We in the modern world are not used to thinking in the long term. It's not taught in our school curriculums, and in our hyper-connected world with its bombardment of information and constant streams of social media vying for our attention, it is hard to imagine the very long term in any sort of tangible sense. We are more accustomed to thinking in terms of quarterly reports, funding rounds, and the next election term. Sometimes we might stretch ourselves to plan a handful of decades into the future, perhaps towards the end of our lives. But most of us don't give much thought to what came before us, the stories and myths of our ancestors, and we tend not to focus on what might happen in one or two or ten generations' time. It is hard to predict what the world will look like in ten years, let alone several hundred. We're living in a time of exponential change. Computing power and the capability of many exponential technologies are doubling in capacity every two years, following a trend known as Moore's Law. With our technologies and anthropogenic systems changing so rapidly, we are caught up in what is happening in the immediate future.

But in truth we are each around on this Earth for just a minute speck of time, and our short-term thinking is putting the viability and survivability of future generations at risk, as well as countless animal and plant species.

So what are the stories and narratives that can help us to join the dots between the past, the present, and the future, and to think in much longer time frames? Any stories that disrupt the illusion of longevity within our own lifetimes can help us think this way. We can take inspiration from the Iroquois tradition of considering the impacts on the next seven generations for any decision that we make, or the five-hundred-year plan put in place by Māori-owned business group Wakatū to be good stewards towards the land and sea. Developing our own versions of these narratives is important, rather than adopting them for purposes that differ in nuance from the original intentions. We can use the practice of narrative foresight, which turns traditional futures thinking on its head from a focus on new technology and predicting the future to a sort of moral imagining in which myths, narratives, and values underpin possible, probable, and preferred futures.[1] From a desired narrative of the future, we can plan backwards to understand what steps we need to take to get there. We can question what policy support may be necessary, which stories will be best to tell, and what kind of framing will be most effective in bringing large swaths of the population with us. Framing a sense of *wonder* and *awe* at the enormity of time helps us to take our place in it with *humility* and *grace*. The concept of Deep Time as outlined above places humans in the context of geological time, and helps to evoke a narrative of something much larger than ourselves.

There is a certain tension between the urgency with which we need to address runaway challenges like climate change and the acidification of our oceans, and the need to think about time in much longer spans. This is a paradox that many systems change advocates struggle with constantly, myself included. There is indeed an urgent need for action, and we need to be cautious not to cross tipping points in the biosphere after which it will be very difficult, if not impossible, to turn back. But we must also recognise that there is much insight to be gained from slowing down and making space for *stillness* and *reflection*, a place from which surprising solutions often arise. We can draw inspiration from the world around us, adhering to the natural rhythms of life. Perhaps we could stop talking about quarterly planning, and instead follow the patterns of the seasons to anchor us to the movement of time, which would have the tandem effect of also helping frame ourselves as part of the natural world once more.

Inside a mountain in western Texas, a 200-foot (61-metre) clock is being built that is intended to work for 10,000 years. Once completed, the bells inside will ring a unique melody when somebody winds the clock, and the chimes have been programmed to not repeat their pattern for ten millennia. When no one is around to wind it up, the clock powers its time-keeping apparatus with energy captured by thermal changes in temperature between day and night on the mountain-top above. The purpose of the clock is to encourage people to think in much longer time frames. I imagine there aren't many things that would make you ponder the future as much as hearing the grandiose chiming of massive bells in an underground chamber, knowing that your distant descendant might stand in the exact spot hearing a different tune, some three hundred generations from now.

The current reality that we have inherited is built upon human stories and narratives. Just as everything around us, all our systems of living, dying, eating, travelling, and merely existing are grounded in myth; the stories that we choose to tell now will frame the world for many years to come. Each and every one of us has a choice. We have the agency to re-author our lives and our societies in small ways, every single day. There is a Greek proverb that says, "A society grows great when old men plant trees whose shade they know they shall never sit in." Are we willing to take actions now while fully aware that we will never see the fruits of our labour? Can we trust in the integrity of some far-off ever after? Are we evolved enough as a species to have faith that our actions now will contribute towards developing a new story of a future untold? For the sake of my children, their children, and countless generations to come, it is my greatest hope that we rise to the challenge.

ABOUT THE AUTHOR

Alina Siegfried is a storyteller, narrative strategist, systems change advocate, TEDx speaker, and award-winning spoken word artist from Wellington, New Zealand. Alina's journey in storytelling and communications has taken her through environmental advocacy, political issues campaigning, social enterprise, crowdfunding, arts, and community development. After winning the New Zealand National Poetry Slam in 2012 (under the stage alias Ali Jacs), she became the first New Zealander to compete in the Women of the World Poetry Slam, held in Minneapolis in 2013. In her role as the founding Communications Lead of the Edmund Hillary Fellowship, she helped bring together a global community of 500 world-leading entrepreneurs, investors, artists, and systems change leaders to develop transformative solutions to pressing global challenges. Alina lives in Wellington, New Zealand.

alinasiegfried.com

ACKNOWLEDGEMENTS

Writing a book is like raising a child, and we all know that it takes a village!

In the first instance, I would like to acknowledge Te Āti Awa Taranaki Whānui and Ngati Toa as the original occupants and stewards of the land upon which this book has been written.

I would like to extend my deepest gratitude to: Mikey Leung, Natasha Akib, and Ants Cabraal for their early support and encouragement; Pekaira Jude Rei for her patience, wisdom, and grace; book contributors Sharn Maree, Sonya Renee Taylor, Devi Lockwood, Topaz Adizes, Tony Green, Janette Searle, and Jee Kim; Janel Atlas and Denise Young who reviewed and provided feedback on early chapters; Kelly Moneymaker and Kehan Miller for their radical honesty, care, and aroha; Zoë Adern who provoked me to lose a whole section and five chapters of the book from an earlier draft; Phoebe Tickell, Alex Evans, Alice Sachrajda, Thomas Coombes, Jon Alexander, Wendy Schultz, and all of the other Narrative Avengers, as well as everyone who sustained me through the early lockdown madness on the NARWHAL (Narrative Working Group

Hopeful and Longterm) calls; Dougald Hine, and all the Homeward Bound family from the Spring 2020 online gatherings; "Harv" and my Collective Intelligence team, particularly Peter Roband who encouraged me to focus on the book full time to get it done and who also designed the cover; my founding patrons on Patreon: Bill Kermode, Hamish White, Alexa Forbes, Kevin Keane, Susan Basterfield, Erin Jackson, and Seed the Change He Kakano Hapai; and Johan Rockström for contributing the foreword.

Thank you also to: Vanessa Ta, Eva Chan, Mark Prain, Raf Manji, Katy Grennier, Lu Davidson, Colin Basterfield, Julio Palafox, Mahala Jay, Kerryn Pollock, Paula Neme, Nungshi Malik, Tashi Malik, Yoseph Ayele, Matthew Monahan, Brian Monahan, Natalie Sisson, Kaila Colbin, Anna Guenther, Richard Bartlett, Kevin Freedman, Allyson Brady, David Bent, Taylor Leedahl, Charles Hamilton, and everyone who ever came to Tonight It's Poetry, Travis Cottreau, Ben Fagan, Michael Gray, Emma Barnes, Michael Howard, Randi Janelle, and anyone who ever came to Poetry in Motion, Tim, Henry, Tai, and the other staff at Le Samourai on Tory Street who kept me caffeinated and nurtured with delicious scones while I occupied their window seat for many, many mornings ... and anyone who I have forgotten (I'm sorry, I appreciate you!)

Thank you to those who have laid foundations before me and inspired my thinking about story, narrative, and systems change over the past ten years: Rebecca Solnit, Adrienne Maree Brown, Joanna Macy, Chené Swart, Chimamanda Ngozi Adichie, Brené Brown, Alex Evans, Johann Hari, Charles Eisenstein, Jodie Jackson, Gaia Vince, George Lakoff, Michael Margolis, Anand Girardardas, Tom Crompton, Marianne Elliot, Jess Berentson-Shaw, Holly Walker, Rod Oram, Jehan Casinader, the late Dick Scott, the late Octavia Butler, the late

Ursula K. Le Guin, the late Donella Meadows, and countless others.

Thank you to my family: Jost and Pauline Siegfried for your unconditional love and for instilling in me a sense of wonder, curiosity, and openness about the world; Nicola Siegfried for being the most loyal and loving little sister anyone could ask for; Tim and Gloria McGirr for letting me turn your spare bedroom into my office for the better part of a year; and most of all my incredible wife and partner in life, parenting, exploration, hilarity, and hard times alike, Mandy McGirr, and our children Taika and Frankie, who teach me daily just how wonderful a world we live in.

GLOSSARY OF MĀORI WORDS

Aotearoa. The Māori name for New Zealand

haka. Ceremonial Māori "dance" combining words and actions used to welcome, challenge, support, or pay respect

hapū. Kinship group, a subsection of the larger grouping of an "iwi"

iwi. Extended kinship group, similar to a band, nation, or tribe, often referring to a large group of people descended from a common ancestor and associated with a distinct territory

kaitiaki. A trustee, custodian, guardian, caregiver, or keeper

kaitiakitanga. The active practice of stewardship, or guardianship, relating to people, land, place, water, culture, and others

mana whenua. The people who carry power of authority over a certain area of land, those who have whakapapa or lineage to that specific area

Māori. The Indigenous people of New Zealand

Mātauranga. Knowledge; systems of knowledge; wisdom

moko kauae. A traditional facial tattoo worn by Māori women as an outward expression of whakapapa

Ngāi Tahu. An iwi who are mana whenua over much of New Zealand's South Island (also sometimes, Kāi Tahu)

Ngāpuhi. An iwi from the Far North region of New Zealand's North Island

Ōtautahi. The Māori name for the city of Christchurch

Pākehā. A New Zealander of European descent, introduced or originating from a foreign country

Papatūānuku. Mother Earth; the Earth Mother

Rangatira. Chief; leader

te ao Māori. The Māori world; the Māori worldview

te Tiriti o Waitangi. The Māori version of the Treaty of Waitangi, signed between Māori and the Crown in 1840 (Note: "te Tiriti o Waitangi" refers exclusively to the Māori text of the Treaty, which has some highly significant differences in wording and meaning from the English version.)

Te Urewera. A native forest and region which holds a lot of significance to the Tūhoe people, and additionally holds legal personhood status. It was formerly a national park before being returned to Tūhoe in 2014.

Te-Whānau-ā-Apanui. An iwi from the East Coast region of New Zealand's North Island

Tikanga. Custom; protocol; practice; correct manner of doing something

Tūhoe. An iwi who are mana whenua to a region in the northeast of New Zealand's North Island

wahine Māori. A Māori woman

waka. A single- or double-hulled canoe

whakapapa. Genealogy; ancestry

whakataukī. A Māori proverb

Tūhoe. An iwi who are mana whenua to a region in the northeast of New Zealand's North Island

wahine Māori. A Māori woman

waka. A single- or double-hulled canoe

NOTES

About This Book

1. Le Guin, Ursula K., "The Carrier Bag Theory of Fiction," The Anarchist Library, accessed June 21, 2021, https://theanarchistlibrary.org/library/ursula-k-le-guin-the-carrier-bag-theory-of-fiction.

2. The DNA of Story

1. Zak, Paul J., "Why Inspiring Stories Make Us React: The Neuroscience of Narrative," Cerebrum: the Dana forum on brain science (The Dana Foundation, February 2, 2015), accessed June 20, 2021, https://www.ncbi.nlm.nih.gov/pmc/articles/PMC4445577/.
2. Milojević, Ivana, and Inayatullah, Sohail, "Narrative Foresight," Futures 73 (2015): pp. 151–162, https://doi.org/10.1016/j.futures.2015.08.007.

3. The Systems Underpinning Our Lives

1. Social Enterprise UK, "Capitalism in Crisis? Transforming Our Economy for People and Planet — SOSE 2019," accessed June 21, 2021, https:/www.socialenterprise.org.uk/state-of-social-enterprise-reports/capitalism-in-crisis-transforming-our-economy-for-people-and-planet/.
2. "The Water of Systems Change," FSG, May 27, 2020, accessed June 20, 2021, https://www.fsg.org/publications/water_of_systems_change.
3. Global Wellness Institute, 2018. *2018 Global Wellness Economy Monitor.* https://globalwellnessinstitute.org/industry-research/global-wellness-economy-monitor-2018/.

4. Humanity at the Crossroads

1. Eisenstein, Charles, *The More Beautiful World Our Hearts Know Is Possible* (Berkeley, California: North Atlantic Books, 2013).
2. "Joanna Macy and the Great Turning," Joanna Macy and the Great Turning, accessed June 21, 2021, https://www.joannamacyfilm.org/.

3. Malik, Nesrine, *We Need New Stories* (London: Weidenfeld & Nicolson, 2019).
4. Evans, Alex, *The Myth Gap* (London: Transworld, 2017).

5. A Four-Year-Old's Guide to Framing

1. Lovins, Amory, *Soft Energy Paths* (New York: Harper & Row, 1979).
2. Lakoff, George, *Don't Think of An Elephant!* (White River Junction, Vt.: Chelsea Green Publishing, 2004).

6. The Value of Values

1. McCandless, David, "Left vs Right (World)," Information is Beautiful (Information is Beautiful, November 25, 2020), https://informationisbeautiful.net/visualizations/left-vs-right-world/.
2. "Perceptions Matter: The Common Cause UK Values Survey," Common Cause Foundation, 2016. https://valuesandframes.org/resources/CCF_survey_perceptions_matter_full_report.pdf.
3. "World Development Report 2017: Governance and the Law," World Bank, accessed June 21, 2021, https://www.worldbank.org/en/publication/wdr2017/.

8. A Collective Hero's Journey

1. Lockwood, Devi, *1,001 Voices on Climate Change* (New York: Simon & Schuster, 2021).

9. Examining Our Stories of Self

1. Brown, Brené, *Daring Greatly* (New York: Avery, 2012).
2. White, Michael, and Epston, David, *Narrative Means to Therapeutic Ends* (New York: Norton Company, 1990).
3. Stewart, Chené, *Re-Authoring the World* (Johannesburg: Knowres Publishing, 2013).

13. Whose Story Is This?

1. Hogan, Heather, "Autostraddle's Ultimate Infographic Guide to Dead Lesbian Characters on TV," Autostraddle, May 2, 2021, accessed June 20,

2021, https://www.autostraddle.com/autostraddles-ultimate-infographic-guide-to-dead-lesbian-tv-characters-332920/.

2. Khan, Al-Baab, Pieper, Katherine, Smith, Stacy, Choueiti, Marc, Yao, Kevin, and Tofan, Artur, June 2021, "Missing & Maligned: The Reality of Muslims in Popular Global Movies," USC Annengerg, June 2021, accessed 23 June 2021, https://assets.uscannenberg.org/docs/aii-muslim-rep-global-film-2021-06-09.pdf.

14. The Subtle Art of Story-listening

1. "Taonga of an Island Nation: Saving New Zealand's Birds." Parliamentary Commissioner for the Environment, May 31, 2017, accessed June 20, 2021, https://www.pce.parliament.nz/publications/taonga-of-an-island-nation-saving-new-zealands-birds/.

2. Kalla, Joshua L., and Broockman, David E., "Reducing Exclusionary Attitudes through Interpersonal Conversation: Evidence from Three Field Experiments." *American Political Science Review* 114(2), 410–25. https://doi.org/10.1017/S0003055419000923

15. Strange Bedfellows

1. Kim, Jee, Hynes, Liz, and Shirazi, Nima, "Toward New Gravity: Charting a Course for the Narrative Initiative," Narrative Initiative, https://narrativeinitiative.org/wp-content/uploads/2019/08/TowardNewGravity-June2017.pdf.

2. Harari, Yuval Noah, *Sapiens: A Brief History of Humankind.* (London: Vintage, 2015).

16. From Me to We

1. "Personal Development Market Size Report, 2020–2027," Grand View Research, 2020, accessed December 22, 2020, https://www.grandviewresearch.com/industry-analysis/personal-development-market/.

17. From Tree to Me

1. Rockström, Johan, and Klum, Mattias. *The Human Quest: Prospering within Planetary Boundaries* (Stockholm: Bokförlaget Max Ström, 2012).

2. Raworth, Kate, *Doughnut Economics* (London: Random House Business, 2017).

19. From Stuff to Enough

1. Jebb, Andrew T., et al., "Happiness, Income Satiation and Turning Points around the World," Nature Human Behaviour 2, no. 1 (2018): pp. 33–38, https://www.nature.com/articles/s41562-017-0277-0.
2. Raworth, Kate, *Doughnut Economics* (London: Random House Business, 2017).

20. From Scarcity to Abundance

1. "Food Production Must Double by 2050 to Meet Demand from World's Growing Population, Innovative Strategies Needed to Combat Hunger, Experts Tell Second Committee | Meetings Coverage and Press Releases," United Nations, accessed June 21, 2021, https://www.un.org/press/en/2009/gaef3242.doc.htm/.
2. "The 2050 Criteria Guide to Responsible Investment in Agricultural, Forest, and Seafood Commodities," WWF, accessed June 21, 2021, https://c402277.ssl.cf1.rackcdn.com/publications/458/files/original/2050_criteria_final_low_res_online_viewing.pdf?1348517472/.
3. "Food Wastage Footprint: Impacts on Natural Resources — Summary Report," FAO, accessed June 21, 2021, http://www.fao.org/3/i3347e/i3347e.pdf.
4. "We Could Power The Entire World By Harnessing Solar Energy From 1% Of The Sahara," Forbes, September 22, 2016, accessed June 21, 2021, https://www.forbes.com/sites/quora/2016/09/22/we-could-power-the-entire-world-by-harnessing-solar-energy-from-1-of-the-sahara/?sh=60009c99d440.

21. From Competition to Collaboration

1. "Mexican Farmer's Daughter: NAFTA Destroyed Us," CNNMoney (Cable News Network), accessed October 6, 2021, https://money.cnn.com/2017/02/09/news/economy/nafta-farming-mexico-us-corn-jobs/index.html.

25. From Now to Forevermore

1. 36. Milojević, Ivana, and Inayatullah, Sohail, "Narrative Foresight," Futures 73 (2015): pp. 151–162, https://doi.org/10.1016/j.futures.2015.08.007/.

www.ingramcontent.com/pod-product-compliance
Lightning Source LLC
Chambersburg PA
CBHW021243060726
47590CB00005B/1876